W0259814

GOING PUBLIC

ADVANCE PRAISE FOR *GOING PUBLIC*

'Through much of his career as a civil servant, U.K. Sinha was intimately involved in the development of capital markets in India. He then served as chairman of the Securities and Exchange Board of India. This book offers a ringside view of the challenges he faced, including the restructuring of the Unit Trust of India, and his battle against fraud, market manipulation and rogue financial firms. It is a must-read for anyone interested in India's financial development'—Raghuram Rajan, former governor of the Reserve Bank of India

'This book by a respected policymaker is a remarkable insider's account of the financial sector. It is enjoyable, educative and an easy read on a complex subject of contemporary interest and is compulsory reading for policymakers and scholars in public policy. Capturing both the dark and bright side of financial sector, it has a unique blend of anecdotes, case studies, analyses and observations. The book has achieved a remarkable balance between the breadth and depth of coverage'—Dr Y.V. Reddy, former governor of the Reserve Bank of India.

'A masterly presentation of the leadership challenges in capital market development from one of India's foremost public professionals. U.K. marshals over three decades of experience within and outside the government to weigh in on the major policy issues in financial sector regulation. Alongside, he weaves in his very engaging personal story with characteristic candour, integrity and restraint'—Dr D. Subbarao, former governor of the Reserve Bank of India.

'U.K. Sinha is undoubtedly among the most experienced and well-informed financial experts in the civil service. He has had the unique experience of managing the Unit Trust of India (AMC) and the Securities and Exchange Board of India, and handling policy issues in the Capital Markets division of the ministry of finance. Having been there and having done it all, Sinha has the best credentials to author a comprehensive and insightful overview of issues in the corporate bond market, regulatory reform and the rather-delicate relationship between regulators and the government. In *Going Public*, he has deftly narrated the dexterity and competence with which he handled very sensitive issues. *Going Public* lucidly explains a host of challenges in the capital markets that face regulators and government. *Going Public* is a must-read for practitioners, regulators and policy framers'—Vinod Rai, former comptroller and auditor general of India.

'U.K. Sinha's *Going Public* offers interesting insights from his versatile career as a bureaucrat, corporate leader and regulator. The book lucidly, yet deftly, addresses the complex web of relationships between the financial sector, government and regulators. For anyone interested in the evolution of India's financial system, there are invaluable lessons to learn from Mr Sinha's sagacity'—Deepak Parekh, chairman, HDFC

'This is an amazing book. It is a story of how one of the largest countries in the world has been taken to the forefront of emerging capital markets by smart and talent people with both the vision and hands-on experience at the grass-roots level to navigate through the complexities of bureaucracy and human ingenuity. India will have one of the largest capital markets in the world. It takes great patience, resilience and attention-to-detail to build these foundations. Chairman Sinha demonstrates how institution-building with independence, professionalism and integrity is key to protecting investors' savings'—Dr Andrew Sheng, Distinguished Fellow at Fung Global Institute, Hong Kong

'U.K. Sinha, who served as the chairman of the Securities and Exchange Board of India (SEBI) from 2011 to 2017, is among the most distinguished regulators of India. As a member of the International Advisory Board of SEBI, I witnessed first-hand his impeccable command of every single issue we discussed, as also the professionalism of his team. *Going Public* is an engaging account of the developments in India's capital market, the challenges it throws at policymakers and how a determined and committed regulator can bring about change that is long-lasting and growth-enhancing. A must-read book for anyone interested in the capital market and its regulation, especially in a fast-growing developing country'—Arvind Panagariya, professor of economics, School of International and Public Affairs, Columbia University, New York City

'With his vast and varied experience as a policymaker, market practitioner and a proactive capital market regulator, U.K. Sinha's *Going Public* is a must-read for both public policy practitioners and aspirants. Written lucidly, the contents cover a large swathe of modern Indian economic history. Future regulators will benefit from the insights and lessons in it, as the Indian financial sector continues to evolve and attain globally comparable depth and complexity'—Rajiv Kumar, vice chairman of NITI Aayog

'As a bureaucrat, U.K. Sinha always wanted to make the most of what was on his plate. As the boss of India's oldest mutual fund, he focused on developing products and spreading in unchartered territories. As the market regulator, he picked his battles and took them to their logical end. A Securities and Exchange Board of India chairman, with two extensions and a six-year tenure, Sinha had to fight five public interest litigations in India's highest court that challenged either his appointment or extension of terms. The graphic narration of how he took on India's largest shadow bank, Subrata Roy's Sahara India Financial Corp. Ltd, is gripping. *Going Public* is the story of the development of India's financial sector and capital markets—warts and all—seen through the eyes of a bureaucrat, a fund manager, and a regulator adept at solving crises and quietly taking on the high and mighty'—Tamal Bandyopadhyay, senior journalist

'U.K. Sinha cut his teeth as an IAS officer in Bihar's toughest zones. We presume it prepared him for the work he did decades later as one of the brilliant crop of Indian economic bureaucrats. *Going Pub*lic is as much an IAS memoir as a must-read insight into the mystifying world of finance and market regulation, and indeed some scam-busting, from Pearl Plantations, to Rose Valley and Saradha Chit Fund, to Sahara'—Shekhar Gupta, chairman and editor-in-chief of The Print

'This is an absolutely fascinating book. Not only does it offer an insightful account of how his career has developed and how he came to play such an important role in the development of Indian capital markets but it also provides an exceptionally informative overview of the functioning of a regulatory institution and the challenges that it faces. I believe that many regulatory agencies around the world can learn valuable lessons from a careful study of the book'—Prof. Colin Mayer, author and professor at University of Oxford

'Anyone interested in pursuing a career in the capital markets of India would be well-advised to carefully study U.K. Sinha's excellent book, *Going Public*. In this easy-to-read volume, Mr Sinha takes us from his early days as a schoolboy in remote Gopalganj, through his various postings with the Indian Administrative Service, to his rise to chairman of SEBI. Mr Sinha gives us an insightful look into the history of SEBI before a detailed look into some of the most interesting cases and problems SEBI dealt with during his time as chairman'—Blair C. Pickerell, former CEO, Asia, of JP Morgan Funds, HSBC Investment Management, Morgan Stanley Investment Management; and former chairman, Asia, of Nikko Asset Management

'One of India's most respected and successful bureaucrats, Sinha writes a delightfully insightful book about his varied career. The book gives you an insider's view into the working of the Indian financial sector. He illustrates how, to have impact in India, bureaucrats have to navigate the constraints with intelligence but yet understand the limitations with humility. The book is a must-read for anyone with interest in the Indian financial sector'—Janmejaya Sinha, chairman, Boston Consulting Group India

GOING PUBLIC

MY TIME AT SEBI

U.K. SINHA

FOREWORD BY PRANAB MUKHERJEE

PENGUIN
BUSINESS

An imprint of Penguin Random House

PENGUIN BUSINESS

USA | Canada | UK | Ireland | Australia
New Zealand | India | South Africa | China | Singapore

Portfolio is part of the Penguin Random House group of companies whose addresses can be found at global.penguinrandomhouse.com

Published by Penguin Random House India Pvt. Ltd
4th Floor, Capital Tower 1, MG Road,
Gurugram 122 002, Haryana, India

First published in Portfolio by Penguin Random House India 2019
This edition published in Penguin Business by Penguin Random House India 2024

10 9 8 7 6 5 4 3 2

ISBN 9780670092413

Typeset in Adobe Caslon Pro Manipal Technologies Limited, Manipal
Printed at Replika Press Pvt. Ltd.

www.penguin.co.in

To my granddaughters, Inaya and Sahana:
my biggest source of joy

Contents

Foreword

Pranab Mukherjee

8 November 2019

The financial core of the country is a large and complex system comprising several organizations and supervisory institutions dealing with banking, insurance, pension, securities market, etc. Most people in India have only a vague idea about the securities market or its regulator, SEBI. Financial literacy and awareness about the market have generally been low. This is one of the main reasons why a tiny fraction—approximately 3 per cent—of the financial savings of the Indian households goes into the market. The general impression used to be that the market was controlled, and often manipulated, by a small band of market players and it was better to keep out of it. Sentiments have started changing in the last decade. SEBI was created with the task of protecting the interests of investors, regulating the market and also developing the market. Its efforts have led to the creation of a stronger supervisory mechanism and higher level of confidence in people's minds.

In this book, U.K. Sinha takes the readers through the evolution of different institutions dealing with the market—such as stock exchanges, mutual funds, foreign portfolio investors, etc. in the country. Emergence of the regulatory framework, the challenges which were faced on the way, the mishaps that took place once in a while and the remedial action taken by the government are worthy of narration to any educated Indian or outsider. Successive governments took policy action to empower SEBI, but often not ahead of time. The journey has not been smooth. Sinha's book captures the interplay of different forces working to create obstacles and delays and how the same were tackled.

Sinha is the right person to tell this story. Not only has he observed the development from different vantage points, but also has he played multiple roles in shaping the developments in the markets: first, when he was heading the Capital Markets division in the ministry of finance, then as a chairman and managing director of UTI mutual fund and, finally, as chairman of SEBI. This book is an incisive analysis of the developments as well as the factors behind the changes.

He first came to my notice when he assisted the finance minister and me during UPA-I in our efforts to convince the left parties to support the Pension Funds Regulatory and Development Authority (PFRDA) bill in the Parliament. He came across as a thorough and mature official who had understood the international and domestic nuances of the issues very well. It is a different matter that the bill could be passed only in 2013. Another occasion was when I was heading the group of ministers (GoM) dealing with import of wheat in 2007. Sinha—who was then in UTI—had been appointed by the government to head an expert group for hedging in the international grain market. The group was able to quickly study different dimensions of the issues, evaluate options and present to the GoM a cautious action plan that resulted in substantial gain for the country. Besides, the group created a strong knowledge-base which could be used for hedging in any other commodity in future. When I became the finance minister, the issues of foreign portfolio flows had assumed significance. I appointed Sinha to head a working group on this subject. The report which he submitted in 2010 formed the basis of subsequent reforms in the sector and is guiding the policies even now. As finance minister, I had no hesitation in recommending his name for appointment as chairman of SEBI, when a high-powered committee headed by the cabinet secretary proposed the same.

The book narrates the reforms in mutual funds, in the primary market, in surveillance, in administration of stock exchanges and introduction of new regulations for FPI, AIFs, REITs and InvITs and municipal bonds. It is heartening to note that the steadfast approach of SEBI in regulatory matters led to success in all the cases in different courts—right up to the Supreme Court. The book provides a detailed insight into the developments in multiple courts, as well as the legislative changes brought about by the government to tackle various related issue in future.

The book is an important part of the history of the financial sector in India, and an important read for all those who seek a better understanding of the forces that often try to derail reforms, and how those efforts can be thwarted by an alert institution working with openness and transparency.

Introduction

My two-and-a-half-year-old granddaughter, Inaya, was excited to visit the SEBI office on Independence Day. She believed that everybody, including her parents, worked in companies. At home she was always curious to know what my 'company', SEBI, the Securities and Exchange Board of India, does. When she went to the office and interacted with several invitees and staff members, she proudly announced that she had understood what my 'company' actually did. Her finding was, 'Your company is the "police" for all companies.'

A few months after being appointed the chairman of SEBI, I was invited to address a group of students and faculty. The host introduced me to the audience as the chairman of SBI! Similar to many, State Bank of India, or SBI, came to his mind more naturally than SEBI.

Such incidents got me thinking that people needed to know more about this organization that is crucial to the financial sector. It is important to know why it was created, its functions, and how it touches the life of an ordinary person. Its relationship with the government and its role in the development of the economy are all matters that should be readily understood by the public. Today, SEBI is one of the most powerful regulators in the world. Its voice and views are received with respect in the global body of regulators. The World Bank and the IMF commend it for all the reforms it has implemented. Other new-generation fellow regulators in the country look upon it as a model they would like to follow.

But the journey of SEBI has not been smooth. It has been one of struggle and fighting for existence. In about the first decade of its existence, it was known more for its lapses: how scams in stock exchanges couldn't be kept in check, how initial public offerings were manipulated or how retail investors felt frustrated that their grievances were not redressed by SEBI. The action it took across different but similar cases was inconsistent. Orders passed by SEBI were set aside by the appellate tribunal, SAT (Securities Appellate Tribunal), more often than they were upheld. SEBI was counted as a toothless tiger.

From brokers to regional stock exchanges—SEBI was on a collision course with almost everyone, and often with little success. Everybody—including the media—had very little consideration for the fact that it was a young organization. Initially, the issue was that it did not have its own manpower and had to learn on the job. For example, screen-based trading was introduced without SEBI having the required technical tools and expertise to supervise it. Similarly, the market opened up faster than SEBI could prepare itself to regulate foreign portfolio investors and participatory notes.

SEBI also had to face a shift from government approval on pricing of an initial public offer to a completely disclosure-based, market-determined process without its staff being trained on how to monitor merchant bankers or the disclosures made by companies. It faced tremendous opposition from people whose interests were being affected. In the financial sector, only the RBI and the government held sway. SEBI was treated like an imposter trying to flex its muscles. The brokers hated it. A litigation with them regarding SEBI's jurisdiction could be resolved only by the Supreme Court—after eight years of the SEBI Act being passed by the Parliament. Corporate India didn't like it and others like mutual funds accepted its role only grudgingly.

On top of all this, SEBI's power remained very limited in the initial years.

Things started changing for the better after about a decade, when, after a few mishaps, the government realized the need to empower it. The ministry of corporate affairs—earlier department of company affairs—had the jurisdiction over all companies, and the ministry of finance over all financial markets. Parting with even some of those powers in favour of SEBI took years. When SEBI was given powers to pass quasi-judicial orders, the appellate authority remained an officer in the ministry. It took years to create a separate appellate body—SAT. This hesitation was also reflected in the process of appointing for senior positions in SEBI. The law gave powers of such appointment to the government but the procedure was left unclear. Lack of a transparent process has often been the cause of problems that the organization has subsequently faced. It took more than a decade to have a rule in place.

This book emerged from the need to tell the story of this journey. I have had the chance to observe SEBI from multiple perspectives, from the ministry of finance looking after capital markets and from my role as chairman and managing director of UTI Asset Management Company, to finally as chairman of SEBI. All these roles gave me different access and knowledge to the working of the capital markets in India and how the Parliament, the judiciary, the government and other regulators approached the capital market and linked institutions. I have attempted to tell the story of SEBI and capital markets in India the way I have observed it during these stints. It is not a history of the development of the capital markets, nor a treatise on how these should be regulated. It is more of my first-hand impressions and experiences in dealing with the subject in different roles. I outline the evolution of SEBI I have witnessed and the challenges that were encountered along the way.

It is also important to examine whether the different responsibilities entrusted to SEBI by the Parliament are in conflict with each other or complementary. The fact that SEBI performs executive, legislative and quasi-judicial functions simultaneously brings about added challenges. The book deals with how these different dimensions have played out over time. Through the course of the chapters, the reader will also have the chance to read more about the early part of my life in Bihar and in the IAS, and how my training in the initial years shaped my approach in dealing with issues and challenges in public life. The influences in my early life and the guidance I have received from multiple people in my career in public service have shaped my values and resolve to face a difficult situation. The book would have been incomplete without touching upon these subjects.

The incidents of market misconduct and the UTI crisis of 2001 provided the background of substantive reforms. Many people suffered losses, and the government and Parliament were worried. A joint parliamentary committee made far-reaching recommendations; action was initiated and measures were taken. The book takes a closer look at these measures and how different players enacted their own drama and tried to write their own script. But for some saner voices many reforms would not have seen the light of the day. Many financial institutions have faced difficulties in the past, and the government has implemented measures to restructure these institutions. But the restructuring of UTI has been, by far, the most successful so far. The persons involved, the difficulties encountered and the actions and decisions taken tell a story of their own about the capital markets.

Finally, the internal and external challenges in bringing in reforms and changes in SEBI form an important part of the story. I had five PILs—all in the Supreme Court—filed against my appointment as chairman of SEBI. The tenacity and the ferociousness with which these were lodged and pursued were quite unnerving. It has been unprecedented in the history of public service in India that such concerted attempts have ever been made against any one individual or organization. These attempts to browbeat SEBI began once it had initiated action against the powerful and mighty. Even the Supreme Court came to this inescapable finding in one of its orders. Had the Supreme Court not dismissed these petitions and cast serious doubt on the intention behind these attempts, any individual or organization would have capitulated.

I also hope to tell readers the stories behind some of the attempts to raise unauthorized deposits from large numbers of people, how SEBI dealt with these situations and the challenges that emerged. Those running these schemes were so sure of their power and influence that they did not hesitate to issue advertisements in the media condemning SEBI, challenging it to face an open public debate on TV and calling it names like 'sarkari gunda'. The book is a tribute to the officials of SEBI who went about their task without being affected by these provocations. SEBI had to fight these cases from the district courts right up to the Supreme Court.

In my book, I would also like to throw light on the developmental efforts of SEBI, which never attract serious public attention. For example, it will focus on the efforts made to revive the mutual funds industry, which declined in size till 2012, and where the assets under management have grown from nearly 6 trillion rupees at that time to over 25 trillion rupees in 2019. It is important as more than 280 million small investors today are entrusting their hard-earned money to funds month after month through systematic investment plans. Reforms brought about in different other areas like alternative investment funds and foreign portfolio investors—to name a few—have also been discussed.

I had the occasion to closely observe the relationship between the government and the regulators from multiple angles. While some attempts to encroach upon the regulatory jurisdiction are widely noticed and reported, there are often some surreptitious efforts that remain unnoticed. The book analyses some of these instances along with their implications.

SEBI and the institutions of the securities market that it regulates remain an enigma even for the educated and well-informed individuals today. This is so in spite of the fact that developments in the market have a strong and direct impact on the lives of ordinary people. This book is an attempt to familiarize the reader with the history of the developments in the market, what led to these changes, the role SEBI has played in them, the challenges it faced, and the factors that ensured its independence as well as accountability. I will feel happy if the book succeeds in providing even partial clarity on these questions.

PART I

Early Life, Ministry of Finance and UTI

1

The Early Days

The journey of 180 kilometres from Patna was always full of adventure and unanticipated challenges. One had to cross the Ganga by a steamer to get down at Pahleza Ghat on the northern bank. From there a train took one to Sonepur, where one had to take another one to Chhapra, and then a third to the final destination. Another option at Pahleza Ghat was to take a taxi or bus to Chhapra and travel onwards by another bus. An Ambassador taxi ferrying ten to twelve passengers was not unusual; nor was travelling on the roof of a bus. Each stage of the journey to Gopalganj, my home town, was a test of endurance as well as resourcefulness. Before, the erstwhile district of Saran was divided into three parts in the 1970s, people from Gopalganj would proudly announce that they belonged to the same district where the first president of India, Rajendra Prasad, was born. By the 1990s, the narrative had changed. Gopalganj was recognized as the place of Lalu Prasad Yadav, the erstwhile chief minister of Bihar. Lately, people have recognized it as the home town of the famous Bollywood and TV actor Pankaj Tripathi.

My grandfather was a mukhtar, a class of legal practitioners who were not qualified law graduates but matriculates passing a licentiate examination in law. Mukhtars would practise in the courts of magistrates but they were not allowed to practise in higher courts. Following in his father's footsteps, my father Phuldeo Prasad became an advocate, graduating with a BSc and Bachelor of Law from Patna University. He practised law for a few years but soon left it to join the Quit India Movement, for which he was arrested in August 1942 and sent to Motihari jail. More than a year later, after he was released from jail, he was determined not to appear before the officials and judges of the British government. So he gave up his practice. But he had no particular plan about what he was going to do for a career. The family struggled for the next decade or so while he started multiple small businesses. He was an entrepreneur and a risk-taker. After about five years, he obtained the licence for a travelling cinema. As per the licence conditions, it could operate at one location only for six months and had to move to another place thereafter. In 1958, he finally opened the first permanent cinema hall in Gopalganj in 1958. The fortune of the family turned thereafter. In less than ten years, he opened a cold storage, and added more businesses and properties over time. He was also a very keen sportsman, excellent at football, tennis, chess and bridge. But he didn't just stop at playing all of them; he was also great at bringing people together and organizing them into excellent teams. The small town of Gopalganj created a formidable football team under the stewardship of my father.

His Majesty the District Magistrate

Gopalganj was a subdivisional town sixty miles away from the district headquarters of Chhapra. The visit of the district magistrate (DM) to the town would always be a big event. The roads were swept and sprinkled with water each time; officials and lawyers wore newly pressed clothes. The deputy collector looking after the licencing of cinemas—the cinema magistrate—would personally visit the theatre well before the entry of the DM or his family. As a result of his visit, the cinema hall, which belonged to my father, was cleaned up and all the paan stains were removed.

Most of the economic activities in our small town—as is true of most towns in India—from running a grain shop to an eatery, supplying sugarcane to mills, or dealing in essential commodities, all were at the mercy of the DM. He was the lord and master who could suspend or revoke the business permission. My grandfather and father were enamoured by the power and prestige associated with the office of the DM. We had progressed from having a mukhtar in the family to an advocate, and the desire to rise further was always there. Both my grandfather and father nurtured a wish that someone in the family should become a haakim (a government officer) and an Indian Administrative Service (IAS) officer someday. My elder brothers became engineers, so the hopes and dreams of becoming a haakim fell upon me.

Early Education

I began my education in a government school that was run on the same principles as that of Mahatma Gandhi's basic school. It was located in a teachers' training institution and was part of an experimental school where teachers could be trained. There was no furniture for the children to sit on. Everyone was expected to bring boras (sacks) for this purpose. Only the teachers had the luxury of wooden chairs and tables. From there I went on to study at the VMMHS School, a government higher secondary school. Here I was encouraged to participate in a whole lot of extracurricular activities and look beyond just academics. I began to take part in recitation contests, debates and public speaking.

In the 1960s, there was a national magazine called *Kishore Bharti*, which was meant for students of high schools and colleges. They would conduct an all-India essay competition, inviting entries from institutions across the country. In 1967, I participated in it and was fortunate to win the first prize in the entire country. It really boosted my self-confidence at the time and gave me my first taste of success. I still remember the award ceremony in Patna, where the Deputy Chief Minister Karpoori Thakur handed me the award.

College Life

After school, I studied physics as part of my graduation and post-graduation from the Patna Science College. In 1972, in the first year of our postgraduate classes, a number of our friends were answering the State Bank of India (SBI) exam for the post of probationary officer (PO). I appeared for the same exam and was selected for the job in 1973. However, I wanted to complete my post-graduation, and so for almost a year I stayed in the hostel while working at SBI.

You Are an IAS

My father and grandfather's wish that I become a haakim was always on my mind. I prepared for the Union Public Service Commission (UPSC) exam while I worked at SBI. The UPSC exams were conducted in the month of October at that time. I had opted to answer the exam at the Patna centre since I was working there. In late September 1975, Patna faced an unprecedented flood. The river Sone had breached its embankment, and water entered the town. As the Ganga was also swollen, the town remained flooded for more than a week. This was hardly ten days before the exam commenced.

I moved from one place to another to avoid the flooding. I finally stayed with my sister in her house in Rajendra Nagar until the water receded and I could move back to my accommodation. Thankfully, on the day of the exam, I managed to reach the centre, and the written exam went well.

I waited anxiously for the result, which came out early next year. This was followed by an interview. The final result was due to come out in May. It was tough to wait those few months to find out if I had made it or not. In the 1970s, the complete results of the UPSC exams were published in newspapers. The tradition was to announce the results on a Saturday. I learnt that the Press Trust of India (PTI) had a teleprinter facility that would receive the results the previous evening. From there, the results were sent to newspapers for publication the next day. Late evening on one Friday, my friend Madan Mohan Jha and I went to the PTI office and requested the elderly gentleman sitting there to let us know the outcome. Thankfully for us, he agreed. I held my breath as he went through the teleprinter message. Finally, he got up, shook my hand and said to me, 'You are an IAS.'

Kolhan Superintendent

The IAS training was a combination of institutional training in the Lal Bahadur Shastri National Academy of Administration (LBSNAA) in Mussoorie and on-the-job training in districts. I was allotted my home cadre of Bihar, and for the district training, the state government sent me to Chaibasa, now in Jharkhand, the headquarters of Singhbhum district. Mantreshwar Jha was the deputy commissioner and Rameshwar Oraon, the superintendent of police. Both of them were very helpful during my stay.

After a couple of weeks, I received an order notifying me to work as the Kolhan superintendent. I did not know where

Kolhan was nor what the superintendent was expected to do. Later I learnt that certain parts of the district that had a dense forest cover, predominantly tribal population and difficult terrain were the last ones to accept British suzerainty in the nineteenth century. A Major Wilkinson, who had led British forces into Kolhan, had entered into an agreement with the tribals there, promising to respect their cultural and legal traditions. As a result, 'Wilkinson's Rules' became the guiding principles for the settlement of disputes. On matters such as matrimony, inheritance or other civil disputes, the courts had no jurisdiction. Instead, matters were to be raised before the court of the Kolhan superintendent. A very powerful provision in the rules was that legal counsel from outside was not allowed, and parties had to present their cases personally, without the aid of a legal representative. Thus, my job involved listening to family disputes about inheritance, adoption, and division of property among others. The appeal lay only with the deputy commissioner. This stint gave me a deep understanding of the inner workings of the tribal society in Kolhan. It equipped me for my future assignments, when I had to be a patient listener to the various points of view and take a final just call.

After completing my training I received a notification that I had been appointed as the subdivisional magistrate of Jamshedpur in July 1978.

Slag Pickers' Society

Within a month of my moving to Jamshedpur, I was faced with a very unfortunate situation. Early one morning, information reached me that seven young tribal children had drowned in the swollen Subarnarekha river.

Tata Iron and Steel Company (TISCO) used to award contracts for the removal of slag from its blast furnaces.

The company would pay the contractor to have the material removed and dumped in a landfill near the river. Some of the slag that was removed was sold by the contractor to different users. Tribal women and children were entrusted with the task of picking up different materials from the dump and segregating these as per their size and content. The slag pickers were ill-treated and exploited by the musclemen of the contractor, often leading to protests and tension. On that day, a serious fracas had developed. The contractor's men had assaulted the slag pickers. Fearing for their lives, the children had tried to run away, but finding no escape in sight, seven of them had jumped into the swollen river and drowned.

My first reaction, of course, was to ensure that strict punitive criminal action was taken against the transport contractor and his employees. However, I also wanted to make sure that we took measures to address the deeper needs of the tribal society. So I formed a cooperative society, of which the first condition was that 100 per cent of its members were to be tribals. We persuaded the TISCO management to award the contract for removing slag to this society at a token amount of Re 1. As the subdivisional officer, I became the cooperative society's ex officio chairman. We had the government allot a piece of land to this society for their work. Within a year of its formation, the society had set up a dispensary, a school and a crèche for the young children. I would visit the work premises every day for several months. The account-keeping was supervised by trained people, and I would check it regularly. My officers too used to frequently visit the place. It was ensured that the sale of the material took place through an open and transparent system. Security too was provided at the site to ensure that there was no outside influence or use of muscle power. The provision of basic facilities such as healthcare, crèches and education for family members and group activities with society members ensured that there was a sense of ownership and pride among the people. The society members got paid fairly for their work and there was no favouritism. Run on sound financial principles, the society very soon developed substantial surplus and revenue. I am told that the society is running successfully to date and continues to work towards the betterment of the tribal society.

Giridih and Patna

I had a few postings in between before I became the deputy commissioner of Giridih (now in Jharkhand), the home district of then chief minister Bindeshwari Dubey, in 1985. I had a very satisfying stint there for two and a half years. The district was consistently evaluated as number one in the implementation of development programmes. We managed to provide the most number of schools and houses for the poor. We also conceptualized and implemented an innovative scheme to supply drinking water from an abandoned coal mine in Giridih. I was proud of the modern stadium and central bus stand that we managed to construct. The chief minister came to Giridih to inaugurate this bus stand. At the inauguration, he announced that I had been shifted to the most important district, i.e. the headquarters district of Patna.

In many parts of the country, large cities have a separate police commissioner. The system of a police commissionerate did not exist in Bihar then and does not even now. In addition to developmental and revenue administration, the district magistrate of Patna was also responsible for the maintenance of law and order. My stint as DM of Patna created a record of sorts. The DM of the headquarters district was always handpicked by the chief minister. A new person was appointed whenever a new chief minister came in, but I had the unique distinction of working with four different chief ministers during my tenure.

Within a few months of joining, Chief Minister Dubey was shifted to Delhi as a minister in the Union government. He was replaced by Bhagwat Jha Azad, who had spent most of his political career as a member of Parliament in Delhi, and had very limited experience and exposure to the bureaucracy of Bihar. When the changeover happened, I was away from the city in Hyderabad attending a mandatory training programme launched by the then prime minister Rajiv Gandhi called 'PM meets DM'. Under this programme, a group of fifteen to twenty DMs were scheduled to meet and interact with the prime minister for an entire day so that the PM could gain insight into the workings of the grass-roots administration in different parts of the country. I found him to be very sincere and well-meaning in trying to understand the difficulties faced in the implementation of development programmes.

I had never met the new CM Azad before. As I got to know him, I realized he was a fair person. He must have received reports from the chief secretary or cabinet colleagues about how things were being handled. One day he called to personally compliment me for handling a very difficult law and order situation when some antisocial elements tried to create a serious crisis during a festival. I also received letters of appreciation from him. Azad began to repose so much confidence and trust in me that he would discuss matters outside of my work with me. Our families also developed a rapport. His wife was a very warm person. I remember she once came to our house when she learned that our child was not well.

Azad was keen to clean up the administration, and he took strong action against those in the cooperative and other similar institutions trying to serve their own ends. As a result, his partymen succeeded in projecting him in the eyes of the high command as an arrogant and unpopular person. He lost out in these internal political differences and was eventually replaced by Satyendra Narayan Sinha. Sinha was a senior politician who deserved to become the chief minister much earlier in his life. By the time he got the position, he had aged and was not in the best of health. He and his wife, Kishori Sinha, both were from very well-respected families and it showed in their sophistication and cultured manner. Kishori Sinha was also an MP. Their son, Nikhil Kumar, was in the Indian Police Service (IPS) and went on to become the police commissioner of Delhi. Later, he became a member of Lok Sabha and also the governor of Nagaland and Kerala.

Because of his age and background, Satyendra Sinha had a tough time relating to grass-roots politicians. He was not a 24x7 politician, and instead believed in certain timings being honoured, rules being followed, and decorum being maintained. This style did not resonate with his peers. His biggest challenge came when the Bhagalpur riots took place in 1989. As a chief minister, he encouraged the bureaucracy to take all the necessary action at its command in maintaining law and order. However, the bureaucracy had got used to taking orders from the political class even for small matters well within its authority and was found wanting in handling the situation. The riots could not be controlled in time, and the unrest spread to other parts of the state. Sinha's reputation could not survive this incident and he was soon replaced by Jagannath Mishra, the fourth chief minister during my Patna tenure. The job had been very hectic and tiring, and I requested the chief minister to let me go, but the 1989 Lok Sabha elections were due in December. He wanted me to stay on until the elections were over, to which I agreed. After the elections, I again requested the chief minister for a change. He gave me a couple of options and, after my input, made me the managing director of Bihar State Credit and Investment Corporation Ltd (BICICO).

Moving to Delhi

I was keen to move out of the state and work in the government of India. I got an opportunity in 1991 when I was posted in the ministry of human resources and development. For a short period, I worked as the private secretary to Ram Lakhan Singh Yadav when he became a minister in the Central government. He was an MLA from a constituency in Patna, where I had been posted. But I did not like what I saw while working with him. I left the job and proceeded on leave. Later, a number of irregularities surfaced with regard to Yadav, and a criminal case was filed against his son and several officials.

Following that, I got a mandatory posting as joint secretary (JS) (Freedom Fighters' Pension and Rehabilitation) in the ministry of home affairs. K. Padmanabhaiah, a very senior and respected civil servant and a towering personality, was the home secretary. V.K. Jain of the IPS, who had earlier been the director general (DG) of police in Uttar Pradesh, was also working at the ministry as special secretary (Internal Security). Fifty years after Independence, there were hardly any new freedom fighters likely to emerge or migrants from Pakistan to be rehabilitated. So this was a position that hardly saw any major policy or activity. Since I had a lot of free time on my hands, I prepared a comprehensive evaluation of different interventions and proposed structural changes, which others at this desk had not cared to do in the past. The home secretary and the home minister appreciated the effort.

Within a few months, I was shifted from the insignificant position of JS (Freedom Fighters' Pension and Rehabilitation) to the most sensitive desk of JS (Security). JS (Security) was the nodal person for VIP security, security of vital installations, administration of Arms Act and provisioning for the central paramilitary forces. One of the main tasks was to handle the Jain Commission on the assassination of Rajiv Gandhi. Another issue was that because of the disturbances in Jammu and Kashmir, Prime Minister P.V. Narasimha Rao had not visited the state for several years. JS (Kashmir) and I prepared the entire groundwork for the first visit and later assisted him in making arrangements for conducting the assembly polls. The Jain Commission summoned former prime minister Rao to appear before it. I had the opportunity to brief him on the facts of the case for days together before his appearance. His testimony before the commission was a treatise on international relations and foreign policy with neighbouring countries.

The experience of working in districts where the situation was fragile and unrest was always a possibility helped me anticipate difficult situations, take timely action and ensure coordination. I was given three rounds of extension on this post.

Going Back to Patna

I went back to Bihar in April 1997, and had the chance to hold a number of positions such as secretary (Department of Welfare), secretary (Department of Agriculture), divisional commissioner of Patna, and secretary (Road Construction Department). Lalu Prasad Yadav was the chief minister when I came back. Because of the developments in the fodder scam, he had to make way for his wife Rabri Devi, who remained the chief minister until I left for Delhi in October 2000. Rabri Devi had her own limitations in understanding the challenges and nuances of administration of a large state such as Bihar. Mukund Prasad, who was the principal secretary for Lalu Prasad Yadav, continued with Rabri Devi as well. He served her and the state with a very high degree of commitment and sincerity. But for the caution exercised by Mukund Prasad, things could have gotten completely out of control.

While Lalu Yadav was in jail, he was kept at a government guest house close to the chief minister's house, which had been notified as a jail. At the same time, very interesting working arrangements were made. According to the grapevine, files that Mukund Prasad felt could be approved by the chief minister were sent to her residence for signature, but files that required inputs from Lalu Yadav were kept separate, and wrapped in cloths of different colours. When Yadav indicated the line of action, a special order was drafted on Rabri Devi's behalf in the CM secretariat and then sent for her signature.

Ministry of Finance

I finally came back to the government of India and joined the ministry of finance as joint secretary (Banking) in 2000. This assignment gave a definite direction to my career. For nearly the next two decades, I had uninterrupted and continuous exposure to the policy formulations and operations in the financial sector of the country. I was given the charge of financial institutions, debt recovery and credit policy. One of the most important and challenging tasks was to work on the transformation of ICICI Bank into a universal bank. There was no precedent. Several knotty issues, such as meeting priority sector lending targets and statutory liquidity ratios, had to be addressed to the full satisfaction of the Reserve Bank of India (RBI) and the government. All the issues were successfully resolved and ICICI Bank became the second-largest bank in the country.

We wanted to work similarly in the case of Industrial Development Bank of India (IDBI), but because it had been created by an Act of Parliament, approval was required from it for any amendment. The entire process took years. Even today, IDBI has been losing market share. It has a high degree of non-performing assets (NPAs) and has made losses for several quarters. It has also seen criminal cases filed against its officials. What is really regrettable is that IDBI had the best capacity for project appraisal and monitoring of large projects. It had been responsible for setting up several other institutions in the country. For example, when National Stock Exchange of India Ltd (NSE) was set up, it was the first institution to do the parenting. When the RBI wanted to exit from Unit Trust of India (UTI), its shares were transferred to IDBI. Not only did IDBI create Small Industries Development Bank of India (SIDBI), but its personnel also successfully run many institutions in the country, including NSE, UTI, National Securities Depository Ltd (NSDL) and Stock Holding Corporation of India (SHCIL), etc. But differing opinions within the organization about its future, delay in obtaining government and parliamentary approval, and a lack of commitment towards making the change led the organization to its current state.

The Shift from Banking Division to Capital Market Division

From early 2001, there were frequent news reports about irregular activities in stock markets. There were stories about tactics being used by certain people to manipulate the market which only caused its sanctity to be vitiated. Insider trading, unfair trade practices and the misuse of the badla system were to blamed. The settlement system of stock exchanges was breaking down. Surveillance and supervision did not have any deterrence. Things came to a head with the famous Ketan Parekh scam. It also transpired that UTI, the largest player in the market, had failed to meet its redemption obligations, and had difficulty repurchasing Unit Scheme-1964 (US-64) units in

July 2001. This led to a complete lack of faith among millions of Indians who had placed a lifetime of savings in UTI or the market. A joint parliamentary committee (JPC) was set up to look into the Ketan Parekh scam as well as the UTI issues.

The Banking division used to be a part of the Department of Economic Affairs (DEA). It was located in the Jeevan Deep Building on Parliament Street, whereas DEA was in the North Block. Officers used to aspire to move to North Block, the real seat of the ministry of finance. However, as per the practice prevailing at that time, it was very difficult, although the banking division was part of the DEA and had not become a separate department as it is now, namely the Department of Financial Services (DFS). The tenure of the then JS (Capital Markets) was coming to an end in July 2002. Because of the challenges faced by the government on account of the Ketan Parekh scam and the UTI problems, it was a critical position to be filled in. A search was on for someone to handle this responsibility. I got a call from the Finance Secretary C.M. Vasudev to inform me that I had been selected for the task. I moved in as JS (Capital Markets) in July 2002.

2

Handling the UTI Crisis

In my role in the Capital Markets division, I was required to work on all the policy and legislative issues pertaining to the capital market. This included pension reforms and external commercial borrowings. Apart from this, the JPC that had been set up had demanded that the action taken report (ATR) on various points raised by them had to be submitted by the government every six months until such time as they were fully satisfied. My job also involved coordinating the ATRs and responses on behalf of different ministries and regulators to be furnished before the JPC. I was ably assisted by Deputy Secretary Surjit Singh and later by Saurabh Garg. For other matters, I had Chandra Shekhar Mohapatra, Shashank Saxena and a whole lot of talented and dedicated economists and civil servants.

My Association with UTI in Multiple Roles

As it happened, destiny had planned my deep and intensive association with UTI in multiple capacities. In the ministry of finance, I was responsible for the measures to assist the UTI investors, repeal of the UTI Act and its restructuring. The new shareholders of UTI, viz. SBI, Life Insurance

Corporation of India (LIC), Punjab National Bank (PNB), Bank of Baroda (BoB), had been conscious of the difficulties in running UTI Asset Management Company (UTI AMC) in its new avatar and were watching the developments very closely. M. Damodaran had been appointed the chairman of UTI after P.S. Subramanyam was removed in 2001. Later on, Damodaran was given the additional responsibility of chairman of IDBI. In December 2004, he left UTI for IDBI and the post fell vacant. I was a member of the board of UTI AMC as well as of Specified Undertaking of the Unit Trust of India (SUUTI). The shareholders requested the finance minister to lend my services for running the organization. I moved to Mumbai in October 2005 as chairman of UTI AMC. Finally, in my third role, as chairman of Securities and Exchange Board of India (SEBI), I was also responsible for the regulatory regime of the entire mutual fund industry, including UTI.

The first task in the ministry was to draw up an action plan to instill confidence in the investing public that everything at UTI was under control and the interest of investors would not be compromised. In its report, the JPC had made multiple recommendations regarding the workings of the capital markets in general and about UTI in particular.

Ownership of UTI

Not a single share of UTI was ever owned by the government. The UTI Act, 1963, provided that 50 per cent of its shares would be with the RBI, 15 per cent each with LIC and SBI and the remaining 20 per cent with other banks and institutions. Later on, the shares owned by the RBI were transferred to IDBI, along with all the special powers and privileges extended to the RBI. IDBI had the right to appoint the executive trustee and four other trustees while the government retained the right to appoint the chairman, but in consultation with IDBI. The executive committee of UTI consisted of the chairman, the executive trustee and two nominees of IDBI in the trustee board. In the past ten years before the crisis, three out of four chairmen had been from IDBI. Besides, the chairman of IDBI had always been one of the nominees on the UTI trustee board.

The UTI Act also provided that IDBI had the right to call for information, approve the appointment of auditors and issue directions to UTI in certain cases in public interest. As such, it is fair to infer that IDBI had full control over the affairs of UTI. But, unlike the RBI, IDBI is not a regulator. It is a commercial organization and often operated in areas similar to those of UTI. IDBI provided term loans to projects and often subscribed to the equity of the companies it assisted. It also had its own mutual fund. UTI had begun all these activities, although these were not part of the original mandate. As a result, there was competition and a huge conflict of interest between the operations of the two organizations.

Being the central bank of the country as well as the banking regulator, the RBI rightly began to withdraw itself from the ownership and operations of organizations it regulated directly or indirectly, even though it had earlier helped create these entities. The RBI divested in UTI and IDBI, and later also transferred its ownership in SBI. When the RBI exited from these institutions, there was a need to provide strong institutional arrangements for sound management and overseeing. But for decades, there was nobody regulating UTI. According to the JPC, the new dominant shareholder IDBI did not set up any strong structure for overseeing despite having overwhelming control.[1]

The Role of the Government

Up until 1997, there used to be a nominee of the government in the trustee board of UTI, but the UTI Act did not envisage this. In order to accommodate a nominee from the government, one of the nominee slots of IDBI was earmarked. The last two nominees before the crisis in 2001 were P.J. Nayak and Arvind Virmani. This practice was discontinued in 1997. The rationale was that UTI should be a board-driven organization run by experts and without any interference from the government, which was not even a shareholder. The idea of having a nominee of the government via a convoluted arrangement through IDBI was found to be not in line with the general principle of post-economic reforms that the government should distance itself from the day-to-day running of financial institutions. However, the JPC was critical of the decision to remove government nominees, and observed that no particular benefit could emerge from it.

The UTI Act did not provide that the institution's annual report be put forth before the Parliament, or that an audit by the Comptroller and Auditor General of India (CAG) be mandatory. While IDBI had certain rights when it came to UTI, the government had no such powers.

As such, after the nominees were withdrawn, the government had no direct mechanism to understand and assess the true state of affairs at UTI. It could raise questions with IDBI or UTI when something serious appeared in the media or when the same questions were asked in the Parliament, but no alternative arrangements, such as periodic reporting of information through IDBI, were put in place. Thus, when the crisis developed in 2001, it came to light that the government had no mechanism for timely and first-hand knowledge. In fact, it was the stand of the government that UTI had kept it in the dark. On this, the JPC lamented that the government did nothing to emerge from the darkness. After the crisis, Yashwant Sinha reversed the decision over government nominees, and Jaimini Bhagwati from the ministry joined the UTI board in July 2001. After him, I joined the board. Even when the UTI Act was repealed and two new institutions—SUUTI and UTI AMC—were created, I remained on the board of both these newly created organizations.

In spite of the government not having any shareholding or any operational control in UTI, the perception among the public remained that it was a government institution. One contributing factor was that the chairman was appointed by the government, of course in consultation with IDBI, which itself was substantially owned by the government. Another fact that cemented the belief was that UTI had been created by an Act of Parliament, and any changes in the Act required the government's active support before going to the Parliament. Additionally, many instruments and schemes of UTI were eligible for tax exemption. It was for these reasons that the government came under severe criticism when the UTI crisis broke out.

US-64

Unit Scheme-1964 (US-64) was the biggest and most popular scheme of UTI. It was sold and repurchased from unit holders not based on the correct inherent value of the portfolio (net asset value) but on artificial prices fixed by the management. A practice that accentuated this problem was that from 1993-94, when UTI started distributing a dividend to unit holders that was much more than the actual income of the scheme during the year. In some years, a dividend as high as 28 per cent was paid, whereas the actual income during the year was less than 10 per cent. In order to continue this practice, the accounting policy was also changed. The basic principle of distributing a dividend is to utilize the surplus made during the year. Upon changing the accounting policy, the surplus and reserves began to be utilized year after year.[2] Obviously, it was not a sustainable practice.

Guaranteed Schemes

All investors must by now be familiar with the oft-repeated disclaimer, which goes: 'Mutual fund investments are subject to market risk. Please read the offer document carefully before investing.' The value of investments can fluctuate depending upon market conditions, and it is difficult to guarantee what the actual value after a given period, say one or two years, will be. This is unlike a fixed deposit in banks, or small saving scheme run by post offices wherein the repayment of the principal as well as the agreed interest on maturity is guaranteed. This is one of the important reasons why banks are monitored very strictly by the RBI. As a further safeguard, the RBI also runs a Deposit Insurance and Credit Guarantee Scheme (DICGS). In case of small savings, the deposits are guaranteed by the Government of India.

By the same logic, if an assured return is to be provided in a mutual fund scheme, somebody has to provide that guarantee. Mutual funds, which have a very small capital of their own, do not have that financial strength. This is why SEBI insists that if a guaranteed return is to be provided to the investors in a mutual fund, then the sponsors (the institutions setting up the mutual fund) must provide this guarantee. SEBI does not permit mutual funds to offer any assured return unless such a guarantee is provided by the sponsors. However, UTI unfortunately continued to launch assured return schemes (ARS) without its sponsors providing any guarantee. The arguments advanced by UTI was that it had created a fund called Development Reserve Fund (DRF), whose corpus in 1998 was Rs 600 crore, which could provide the guarantee. UTI also felt that DRF would grow at the rate of Rs 125 crore per annum. The JPC later held that the management of UTI had made an erroneous projection about DRF being sufficient.[3] It held the then executive trustee and chairman responsible for making this projection before SEBI. Ultimately, when the crisis of 2001 took place, there wasn't sufficient money in DRF to pay back the investors. What further complicated the problem was, that though in the initial years ARS were launched only for one year, later they were launched for longer terms, thereby exposing UTI to more uncertainty and making it more vulnerable.

All of this propelled the crisis in early 2001 when it was discovered that UTI had no means to meet the shortfall between the amount promised to the shareholders and the actual value of the portfolio. The JPC arrived at the decision that IDBI was accountable for ARS. Its nominees were the ones who had taken the decision. When SEBI asked UTI who its sponsors were so that they could be asked to take up the responsibility, UTI replied that it had no sponsors! Ultimately, it came upon the government to step in and take on UTI's liabilities.

Another irregularity at UTI was its practice of inter-scheme transfer. A mutual fund that runs several schemes can buy or sell the same shares and debentures for its different schemes on a given day. But there are separate rationales for buying or selling a particular share at a particular price on a given day for each scheme. Shares bought for one scheme belong to that scheme and cannot be sold or transferred to another scheme run by the same mutual fund unless there are exceptional circumstances justifying this. There are well-laid-out criteria as to when these inter-scheme transfers can take place. However, it was discovered that the practice of inter-scheme transfer of securities from one scheme to another was rampant at UTI and the directions of SEBI were not being followed. According to the JPC, just within US-64, the inter-scheme transfer was Rs 43,334 crore between 1998 and 2001. What is even more appalling is that many of these transactions had been reversed, i.e. the same shares had been bought back in less than thirty days.[4] Obviously, this practice was being used as window dressing when a particular scheme was having a bad day and needed a more rosy picture to be presented to the public. It is possible that it was also being used to hide the mistakes of fund managers.

UTI was found to be indulging in unwanted and unconnected activities, such as helping Calcutta Stock Exchange (CSE) in March 2001 when they had a payment crisis because certain brokers had defaulted. UTI bought shares of a company that were worthless and as a result provided CSE enough money to meet its settlement requirements. That single transaction by UTI cost it more than Rs 21 crore.

US-64 Erupts

The Ketan Parekh scam and the circumstances around it led to a massive decline in the prices of shares in the market. It was inevitable that shares held by the schemes of UTI, more so US-64, eroded in value. This of course prompted investors to start selling their units to avoid further losses. More and more unitholders came forward seeking encashment of their investments, resulting in an unusually large redemption in US-64 during April–May 2001. As the redemption price (repurchase price) fixed artificially by UTI was much higher than the net asset value (NAV), i.e. the actual value of the portfolio, redemption put even more strain on the scheme. It would have been only a matter of time before US-64 would have had no shares in its portfolio to sell and pay off the unitholders. What exacerbated the public's anger was that preferential treatment was given to large investors such as SBI or ICICI. Both of these banks particularly had nominees in the UTI board. They knew the state of affairs there much before the rest of the world, and were the first to encash their units. On 2 July 2001, the UTI board took the unprecedented step of refusing to pay the US-64 unitholders for the next six months, and suspended the repurchase/redemption.

Warning Signs

The problems at UTI did not emerge overnight in 2001. Warning signs had appeared after the first two decades of its existence, when the mutual fund space had been opened for competition and UTI had lost its monopoly. The fact that UTI was not subjected to SEBI jurisdiction and was simultaneously performing the role of a mutual fund as well as a term-lending institution created worry in the minds of policymakers and market experts. The ministry of finance wrote to UTI as early as 1992 stating that investor protection guidelines of SEBI must apply to it, and it should create an asset management company for its mutual fund functions. In 1993, UTI set up a committee under N. Vaghul, chairman of ICICI, to examine the issue, wherein Vaghul clearly recommended that SEBI's jurisdiction should be extended to UTI's mutual fund schemes. Even the JPC inquiring into the Harshad Mehta related scam offered similar recommendations towards the end of 1993, and the government supported this view. Finally, from 1994, UTI came under the voluntary compliance of SEBI mutual funds regulations for all its new schemes. However, US-64 and ARS remained out of SEBI jurisdiction.

Starting 1996, the RBI started raising concerns about the administration of UTI and wrote multiple letters to the ministry of finance to amend the UTI Act and curb activities such as extending loans and advances, and discounting of bills, all of which were not provided for in the original Act. These services were similar to those provided by banks and term-lending institutions, and actually contributed to lowering the credit discipline in the country. But UTI kept stonewalling reforms. It sent alternative proposals guided by its own assessment of the extraordinary role it was playing in the growth of the economy. The RBI kept reminding the government, but no substantial measures were taken until the crisis in 2001. Another committee set up by UTI to inquire into the affairs of US-64 submitted its report in early 1999, which pointed out several lacunae in the working of UTI. It was official that US-64 had a severe shortfall. The government agreed to subscribe to the public sector undertaking (PSU) shares held in US-64, and a new scheme—Special Unit Scheme-99 (SUS-99)—was carved out. The government provided Rs 3300 crore to buy these shares at face value against their actual value of Rs 1500 crore. Another committee was set up under the chairmanship of Y.H. Malegam to review UTI's competitive position.

UTI had an equity research cell (ERC) of expert financial analysts that was supposed to give advice on buying and selling decisions about a particular security based on research. The JPC commented that the recommendations of the ERC were neglected and overlooked. The Tarapore Committee, which was appointed to look into the investment decisions of erstwhile UTI, identified eighty-nine companies where a substantial amount of money had been invested, but the decisions didn't seem to have been made logically, but had been made for extraneous considerations. The Tarapore Committee recommended a special audit of these investment decisions.

In some cases, it was noted that while one set of logic had been given to buy a security, within four days a contrary recommendation had been made and the same security was sold at a loss. Several other instances of irregularities and unprofessional approach were highlighted.

So there was no dearth of warning signs, expert opinions, and findings of committees. But the operations continued without any structural changes.

Drama around US-64

The practice of a government nominee on the UTI board was discontinued in 1997, but the government and SEBI were expected to be watchful. The UTI management also didn't do much to keep the government informed. On 18 May 2001, Subramanyam, the then chairman of UTI, wrote a letter to the finance secretary. Even in this letter, there was no mention of the impending crisis. On the contrary, it was mentioned that the NAV was Rs 9.50, and based on certain projections, the scheme was likely to earn more by 30 June and be in a position to declare a dividend of 12 per cent and maintain an NAV of Rs 10. It was discovered later that this communication from the chairman was never processed in file by the joint secretary or anyone else and presented before finance minister Sinha. Subramanyam met Joint Secretary Bhagwati in the last week of June. According to him, he appraised Bhagwati about the deteriorating condition and requested him to apprise the finance secretary and the finance minister. But, according to Bhagwati, Subramanyam met him without any prior appointment. It was a casual and informal conversation. Since 30 June and 1 July fell on a weekend, it appears that neither the finance secretary nor the joint secretary informed the finance minister until 2 July, the date of the board meeting.

The decision to stop the encashment of US-64 unit was a step that shocked the entire capital market in the country. The government was soon to come in for serious criticism about its own role.

Restructuring of UTI

It was in this environment that I was brought to the Capital Markets division after Bhagwati's term got over. Sinha had been moved to the post of minister of external affairs while Jaswant Singh became the new finance minister. The mandate given was to find a structural solution to the problems of UTI, but to ensure that investors did not suffer. Singh gave us complete freedom to find a solution. He advised that among the people who could provide guidance, Bimal Jalan, the then governor of the RBI should be consulted. We travelled to Mumbai to meet him.

Jalan was very liberal with his time. He placed many options on the table and finally advised that a 'good bank, bad bank' approach would be most suitable. The idea was that all schemes such as US-64 (i.e. ARS), wherein the government was explicitly or implicitly a guarantor, could be brought into a separate institution. We called it UTI-I at the time. All the other schemes that were in keeping with SEBI mutual funds regulations could be grouped under a separate entity, which could then be registered as a mutual fund and be regulated by SEBI. Obviously, in this segregation, both the liabilities and assets of the respective schemes would go to the separate entities.

We kept Damodaran informed of this development. Without his help, this scheme could not have been implemented. One of his demands was that he be allowed to lead both the institutions, i.e. UTI-I and UTI-II. The finance secretary and I also felt that bifurcation of such a large organization initially required one single command; otherwise the whole exercise might be impeded by differences in personalities and inter-organizational disputes. The government readily agreed to this suggestion.

S. Narayan, the finance secretary, kept himself closely updated on this development and provided all the support to get proposals cleared at the level of the minister or in the cabinet. Narayan was an esteemed civil servant. He also enjoyed the trust of Singh and senior officials in the Prime Minister's Office (PMO). He was a hard taskmaster but he always fully backed his team.

Nationalization of UTI

We were careful not to say so, but the repeal of the UTI Act and the creation of two institutions was, in reality, the nationalization of UTI. However, projecting this reform measure as nationalization would have been regressive and anti-reformist. But, in effect, that is exactly what it was. By the provisions of the UTI Repeal Act, the whole entity of erstwhile UTI came to be owned by the government. Then the schemes were bifurcated into UTI-I and UTI-II. All ARS were part of UTI-I, which was renamed SUUTI. It had to have an administrator and a board of advisors. Damodaran was made the first administrator. All the liabilities and assets of the various schemes, such as shares, debentures or real estate, also went to SUUTI. The schemes compliant with SEBI mutual funds regulations became part of UTI Mutual Fund. A separate company, UTI AMC, was created to manage these schemes.

In order to provide confidence to the larger market it was important that the new shareholders of UTI AMC were financially strong entities. SBI, LIC, BoB and PNB were chosen for this purpose. However, since all of them had their own existing mutual funds, special dispensation had to be sought from SEBI for them to have a stake in UTI AMC. G.N. Bajpai, the SEBI chairman, was very supportive of this course of action. A set of guidelines were issued, basically putting restrictions on the four institutions from having their employees on the board or management of UTI or making investments in the schemes. It was also expected that the shareholding would be a temporary arrangement.

The new shareholders paid the government Rs 1296 crore as the value of UTI Mutual Fund. I became a member of the board of directors of the new UTI and also a member of the advisory board of SUUTI. SUUTI was a lean organization by design. However, the schemes that had been transferred to SUUTI had thousands of investors, most of them belonging to the retail category. Their interests had to be safeguarded, and their service requests had to be attended to. A service agreement was signed to allow UTI AMC to manage the schemes of SUUTI and service its investors. To avoid pressure on SUUTI to sell its shares or debentures, the strategy envisaged was to motivate the investors to remain within the schemes. For this purpose, five-year bonds, wherein the income of the bondholder was kept tax-free, were issued by SUUTI in FY 2002-03 and designed such that investors could get higher returns than the prevailing market rates. These were guaranteed by the Government of India, so as to provide comfort to investors. This helped postpone the immediate pressure on UTI and the market. The size of these bonds was worth nearly Rs 15,000 crore.

The Government Makes Money

The two-fold intention of the government was (i) that investors don't suffer any loss and (ii) there is no volatility in the market because of the forced sale of shares and debentures of UTI schemes. As the market continued to consolidate further, the assets (shares and debentures) of the SUUTI schemes gained much higher valuation than the payout for tax-free bonds. For quite some time it remained a sensitive issue as to how, by using the powers of the Parliament for nationalization, the government could make money at the cost of investors. Just three investments of SUUTI's schemes in UTI Bank (now Axis Bank), Larsen & Toubro (L&T) and ITC were several times more than the entire commitment of the government in the tax-free bonds. But nobody raised these issues seriously, primarily because the investors of erstwhile UTI were large in number, dispersed and had, at the least, got back their capital. Institutions such as IFCI, SCICI, Industrial Investment Bank of India (IIBI), IDBI and UTI have all faced problems in the years they've been in operation, and the government has had to intervene in these cases before, but the UTI restructuring has by far been the most successful.

The government and the shareholders provided complete freedom in running UTI AMC, and selecting a new board of directors. The first task was to deal with the large number of employees on the rolls of UTI, which was vastly disproportionate to the size of funds that UTI had. To remedy the issue, Damodaran launched a voluntary separation scheme (VSS). It was resisted by employees, but he was firm about it. The government also provided money to meet the VSS expenditure.

With all the adverse perception about the organization, the morale of the executives was very low. Damodaran did not let it slide and took up a number of measures, including a provision of fast-track promotion for meritorious staff. But this ran into its own set of issues because those used to the liberal seniority-based promotion were not prepared to be bypassed by junior members. The employees were also offered performance-based bonuses, but again those denied the bonuses became restive. The crux of the matter was that having been used to working in a culture of diluted and undefined accountability for decades, many employees were resistant to new practices.

3

Ministry of Finance (Capital Markets Division)

Amendment to the SEBI Act in 2002

Besides restructuring UTI and providing a long-term solution to its problems, the other important task was to amend related laws so as to empower SEBI in dealing with emerging challenges. Attempts to amend the SEBI Act had been going on for years, but the Ketan Parekh scam and the JPC report brought urgency to the exercise. It is not unique to India that changes in the laws governing stock exchanges and share market have been enacted only after major incidents of misconduct have taken place, and not preemptively or when these problems were still much smaller and more manageable. The setting up of the Securities and Exchange Commission (SEC) and the passing of the SEC Act in the USA only took place after numerous examples of misconduct were discovered during the Great Depression. Similarly, the 2001 crisis led to the Sarbanes–Oxley Act, and the 2008 crisis led to the Dodd–Frank Act. Many other countries followed suit and strengthened their laws governing the securities markets after the crises.

The SEBI Act had been passed in 1992, but it had limited powers in prohibiting continued offences or investigating violations. It could demand records or information from a limited set of entities such as intermediaries, banks and companies listed on the stock exchanges, and its writ did not extend beyond this set. The JPC strongly recommended that the powers of SEBI be enhanced. The amendment in 2002 substantially expanded the scope of its authority. SEBI could then designate one of its officers as an investigation authority who could not only demand the production of records from 'any person associated with the securities market in any manner' but also keep such documents in its custody up to six months. In case of reasonable suspicion that documents may be destroyed, SEBI was also authorized to conduct search and seizure after getting approval from a court. The amendments also built in measures that would prevent harm to investors, authorizing SEBI to pass interim orders during investigations, suspend trading, restrain a person from trading, or even suspend an officer of a stock exchange. The quantum of penalty that it could impose was also substantially enhanced.

But, in spite of the JPC's recommendation, getting these amendments through was not easy. There were issues of turf and jurisdiction between the department of company affairs, now called ministry of corporate affairs (MCA), and SEBI. Quicker enactment could be ensured because Singh became the minister of finance and also the minister for the Department of Company Affairs. Once he was convinced about the need for changes, all the objections of the Department of Company Affairs were cleared. It was decided that the ordinance route be chosen instead of the formal passage of amendment through the Parliament. The trust that Singh enjoyed with the then prime minister Atal Bihari Vajpayee also helped. Another person who contributed significantly was Arun Jaitley, the law minister. He personally devoted time to fine-tune many provisions. One important idea he introduced was that the appeal against the orders of Securities Appellate Tribunal (SAT) could be filed directly with the Supreme Court, bypassing the role of high courts on the appellate side. This greatly enhanced the prestige of SAT and also of SEBI. Later, when the bill was placed before the Parliament, it was passed more easily because the Parliament had already grappled with the matter through the mechanism of the JPC.

The 2002 amendment in the SEBI Act was a game-changing amendment. The organization gained substantial powers and support from the Parliament. In later years, this charter of amended powers came in handy in dealing with several instances of attempted misconduct or fraudulent activities.

Law Relating to Stock Exchanges

In a financial system, stock exchanges perform a greater role than even banks. The slightest loss of trust in the stock exchange mechanism can lead to the flight of capital and result in a huge negative impact on the economy. Stock exchanges have traditionally been managed like clubs; members have exclusive rights to enter, manage the affairs of the club, and the privilege of enjoying the benefits of its activities. Similarly, brokers have traditionally had three main rights in a stock exchange—the exclusive right to trade, manage the affairs and exercise ownership rights.

All three rights are mutually shared amongst the brokers. Since the mid-eighties, global consensus emerged that there are inherent risks in the existing system of mutual rights of brokers. The concept of demutualization, where the trading rights, ownership rights and management rights are not mutual and can be allotted to others as well developed and gained ground. During 2001, it was discovered that the president of Bombay Stock Exchange (BSE) had obtained sensitive information from the surveillance department of the exchange about actual shares for which 'buy' or 'sale' orders had been placed, their quantity and prices in the entire order book.[1] This data was not available to other brokers or investors. It was extremely valuable because its timely knowledge can help the broker evaluate the market situation and make handsome gains at the cost of others. During the incidents of 2001, it was also discovered that the IT system of CSE had been tampered with so that an automatic alert about individual brokers falling short of funds was disabled. The system was initially set up to deactivate the terminal of any broker whose margin amount fell below the amount required. This would debar them from further trades and their shares would be auctioned by the stock exchange to realize their dues. But the system in CSE failed and this didn't happen. In March 2001, it faced a serious situation wherein the exchange failed to meet its obligations for settlement. Those who placed orders to buy shares failed to bring the money, and those who sold shares could not produce shares for delivery to buyers. Settlement failure is the worst possible scenario for a stock exchange. It is worse than a bank failing to pay its depositors, and can impact trust in the market as well as the economy in a big way.

In both these cases, brokers who were also part of the management of the exchanges were behind the irregularities. Several other irregularities were also discovered in other exchanges across the country during the same period.

Out of the twenty-four exchanges in the country, three—BSE, Ahmedabad Stock Exchange and Madhya Pradesh Stock Exchange—were an association of persons; nine were companies limited by shares; and twelve were companies limited by guarantees. All, except NSE and Over-the-counter Exchange of India (OTCEI), were non-profit mutual organizations. The JPC also recommended that stock exchanges be demutualized and corporatized. The law governing the stock exchanges, i.e.

the Securities Contracts (Regulation) Act (SCRA), would have to be amended for this to happen. The ministry prepared a proposal where any 'fit and proper' person could have the right to trade on a stock exchange. In order to limit the influence of brokers, it was proposed that the shares held by brokers in the corporatized stock exchange be limited to 50 per cent of the total. Within this, no one broker would hold more than 5 per cent of the shares. The most critical part of the amendment was that brokers would be kept out of the management. Their representation in the board of directors of the stock exchanges would be kept at less than 25 per cent, and they would not be able to occupy critical management positions such as chairman or head of surveillance, IT or listing.

There was an uproar in south Mumbai (where a majority of the big brokers are located) against this proposal. Pressure was applied on the government to desist from this move by appealing to the member of Parliament from south Mumbai and the incumbent minister of the state (MoS) in the ministry of power. She wanted to meet Singh, who had refused to meet the brokers directly. He asked me to meet the MoS (Power) and hear the brokers' representatives. The delegation was led by Vallabh Bhansali, and several objections were raised against the proposal. A key point raised was that brokers would lose all the money that they had invested in buying the ticket from BSE to become brokers. It was alleged that the government was proposing to nationalize BSE and all other exchanges. Nothing was farther from the truth. All the existing brokers were to be offered full value by way of shares in the demutualized exchange. Once I explained the position, Bhansali realized that he and a few others had been misled by other brokers. He took a dignified and fair stand in the meeting. The MoS also didn't have any reason to disagree once all doubts had been cleared. As a last-ditch stand, the brokers reiterated the demand to continue to have a say in the management of the exchanges. This was declined categorically. The firmness with which Singh approached the situation and provided his full support to the demutualization move helped the law be amended immediately. When BSE was listed, the brokers received the full value of their shares, which was several times more than their actual investment of buying the tickets. The whole campaign about nationalization was proven to be wrong!

When I came to SEBI years later in 2011, we formulated the Stock Exchanges and Clearing Corporations (SECC) Regulations. The amended Act provided for up to 25 per cent seats for brokers in the board, but we decided to interpret up to 25 per cent in a certain way and made sure the SECC Regulations expressly provided that brokers would have no representation. The incidents of BSE and NSE in 2001 were still fresh in my mind. I did not want any chance of trading interest compromising the management of the stock exchange.

New Pension System (NPS)

One of the important tasks in the ministry was also to oversee reforms in the pension sector in the country. The Old Age Social and Income Security (OASIS) report had been presented by a group of experts as early as 2000. It made a very strong case for providing social and income security by recommending a defined contribution pension system wherein workers could save regularly for their old age. The group had examined the practices in many parts of the world, including Chile where it had been a success. The experts also determined that the financial burdens of a defined pension scheme for the general public were becoming unsustainable in many parts of the developed world. Post Second World War, governments had shown their strong commitment to provide social security to their ageing population, but the substantial increase in lifespan across the world made the initial projections go haywire and placed additional burden on the government. This resulted in a move towards a pension scheme where the contribution of the employer and the government was defined across the world.

The task of examining and implementing the pension scheme came to the Capital Markets division in the ministry of finance. Pension generally meant a commitment to provide a fixed set of benefits to the retiree, spouse or family, but in a defined contribution system the contribution by the government or employees was decided up front and put aside monthly. Unlike the existing provident funds, the contribution could then be managed in an individual's retirement account, and the individual could track his pension assets. The growing depth of the Indian capital market provided more confidence regarding opportunities where these pension contributions could be invested. The scheme was called the New Pension System (NPS).

At the same time, two important decisions to phase out the old scheme were taken. One was to introduce the NPS as a mandatory defined contribution system for newly recruited government employees. It goes to the credit of the strong leadership of Prime Minister Vajpayee that such a monumental decision that fundamentally changed the retirement benefits of government employees was implemented without any protest. All government employees—except those serving in the armed forces, appointed after 1 January 2004—were no longer entitled to the fixed benefits of a lifelong pension from the government and instead, as outlined under the NPS, the government made upfront additional payments every month as 10 per cent of the salary as employer contribution. The employee also made a contribution of 10 per cent of his salary. Later, the contribution by the government was enhanced to 12 per cent in 2018. The contribution was to be managed by pension fund managers appointed by an independent regulator—Pension Fund Regulatory and Development Authority (PFRDA). The employee has an option to choose amongst multiple fund managers and multiple investment options such as safe and balanced. The new scheme also added on other benefits such as the option to shift the account in case of a change of job. Unlike the existing provident fund scheme where there was a single investment option and opacity in information flow, the employee had full control over his retirement account.

Tax concessions similar to those of a general provident fund or public provident fund were also provided. PFRDA was created through an ordinance in 2003, but with the change of government in 2004, the law could not be immediately passed. I was present for several rounds of discussions with members of the left parties, wherein P. Chidambaram as finance minister and Pranab Mukherjee as the main troubleshooter of the UPA government tried to convince them, but without any success. The bill was passed only in 2013, a full ten years after the ordinance! Except for two states, West Bengal and Tamil Nadu, all other states have voluntarily joined the NPS. PFRDA has now come of age as a regulator. The total assets being managed under the NPS as of 31 March 2019 are more than Rs 3,18,000 crore, and the number of subscribers is more than two crore and seventy-three lakh.[2] On retirement or at the age of 60, the pensioner can withdraw up to 60 per cent of the corpus and the balance 40 per cent is to be utilized to buy an annuity so that lifelong pension can be received. What is satisfying is that the investment options have since inception shown a tax-free compounded annual growth rate between 9.5 per cent and 12 per cent.

Murasoli Maran

Among the multiple subjects allotted to me, one was the foreign exchange desk. With the enactment of Foreign Exchange Management Act (FEMA), the release of foreign exchange for transactions such as medical care and education stood vastly liberalized. Approvals, if required, were delegated to the RBI. However, one area where successive governments found that control over forex could be used as a handy leverage was the power to approve or deny foreign travel to government officials and ministers, including chief ministers of state, MPs and MLAs. Nobody could travel on an 'official' tour without approval under FEMA.

One incident in particular stands out in my mind. The senior leader of Dravida Munnetra Kazhagam (DMK) Murasoli Maran had gone abroad for medical treatment. He was a cabinet minister without any portfolio in the government of India. Unfortunately even the best treatment did not help his condition, and he was in coma for weeks. At some point, there were indications that he would not survive more than a few days. His party decided to bring him back to India so that he could breathe his last amongst his people in his own country. Approval under FEMA was required to release the foreign currency so that he could be brought on a chartered plane.

I was in the midst of a meeting with half a dozen visitors when a bundle of files was brought and kept on my table. One had to develop the habit of regularly looking at the papers kept in the in tray. The moment I saw the heading with Maran's name in one of the files, I realized the gravity of the situation. A delay of even a few hours in granting the approval had the potential of creating an unfortunate situation. Maran had to be brought back alive to India. Stopping all other work, I processed the file, went to the finance secretary and finance minister for their endorsement and sent it to the PMO. I spoke to PMO officials for a quick approval. In the meantime, I rang up RBI officers asking them to keep the sanction letter ready at their end and also to alert the bank that had to actually make available the foreign currency. Meanwhile, Maran's party people and others started making inquiries about the 'delay'. But the entire process was completed in less than an hour. Maran was brought back to India, but sadly he passed away within a few days of coming to Chennai. The finance minister Singh personally thanked me for anticipating the gravity of the situation and acting promptly.

Smelling a File

Public servants deal with multiple issues at the same time. But they have to evolve a sense of prioritization in deciding which issue to tackle first and without delay. A few years before this incident, V.K. Jain had given an important advice to us about 'smelling a file'. His advice was that a public servant should have the knack to distinguish which message, paper or file cannot wait even for five minutes and which can wait for days or weeks. Lack of appreciation of this sensitivity can cause serious harm to the government or the public.

Intelligence reports from multiple sources keep pouring in from different agencies in the ministry of home affairs all the time. Most of these may be vague, but a certain follow-up drill on these reports is prescribed. Jain reminded us of how the famous Purulia arms drop case was handled. An intelligence input was received in the ministry about the likely movement of a cache of contraband and deadly consignment from a foreign country, to be airdropped in the eastern part of the country. Somebody in the ministry should have picked up the phone and alerted the chief secretaries and DGs of police in these states. Instead, the message was transmitted. A prompt reaction would have been to send a coded message or to send a fax. But a junior officer pointed out that rules do not allow 'top secret' messages to be sent by fax. So, following the prescribed procedure but without applying any judgement about the seriousness of the matter, the intelligence report was sent in a double-sealed envelope to the relevant officials by speed-post. The arms drop did take place in Purulia. The speed-post reached the state authorities two days after the arms drop had actually taken place.

Crisis in the Market post 2004 Elections

It is not the duty of the government to supervise or monitor the developments in the capital markets on a continuous basis. But, being accountable to the Parliament, the government has to keep an eye on unusual and big-impact events occurring in the market. My colleagues in the Capital Markets division and I designed a system of capturing developments proactively and alerting the government in time. For example, if there was an important geopolitical development or major economic or financial development that could affect market sentiment and create volatility, the team in the Capital Markets division would analyse the reasons and consequences and inform the higher-ups. It often depended upon the individual finance ministers as to how closely they wanted to monitor the situation. Singh did not want to be disturbed with smaller developments, but Chidambaram was more proactive and did not want to be surprised. We developed a template of reports capturing important domestic and international developments at the end of each day. Depending on the gravity of a situation, matters were reported even up to the prime minister at times.

The Parliamentary elections of 2004 was a time when this system came into use. Unlike the pre-election assessment of the NDA government winning a second term and forming the next government, the results showed that the NDA was going out of power. The new coalition that emerged was led by the Congress and depended heavily on the left parties. The NDA government of PM Vajpayee was credited with reforms such as disinvestment of PSUs, introduction of the NPS, deregulated interest rates, and progress towards dismantling the artificial pricing system for petroleum products. These measures had generated positive sentiments in the market. After the election, people were expecting more such reforms, but the Congress and left parties, which were opposed to these policies, had won the election. From Thursday, 13 May 2004, when the results were announced, some prominent left leaders started making press statements that they would roll back these measures of the NDA government. The unexpected results, coupled with these statements, created panic in the market and led to heavy selling on Friday. The benchmark index Nifty 50 fell by 8 per cent. Senior officials of the ministry and I assembled in the room of Finance Secretary D.C. Gupta and felt that the market needed assurance on policies. We got in touch with the Cabinet Secretary K.M. Chandrasekhar who then contacted Singh and PM Vajpayee. Gupta told me that both felt that having lost the mandate of the people they had no moral authority to take any measure or make any statement, although technically they were still in power.

We approached Dr Manmohan Singh, the Congress leader and former finance minister, to issue some communication to assuage fears about the drastic reversal of economic policies. We thought he was likely to be the finance minister in the new government, but none of us had imagined that within two weeks he would become the prime minister. Singh, with his vast experience of working in the government, understood the situation and appreciated the concerns of the finance ministry officials. He promised to check with Congress President Sonia Gandhi. The next day, he did issue a statement, but as they were not yet formally in power and would be dependent on the support of the left parties, the statement was diplomatically mild and did not make any categorical assurance. It did not bolster sentiment in the market as was required, and the mood remained grim. G.N. Bajpai, who was the SEBI chairman at that time, writes in his book *A Game Changer's Memoir*, 'Optimism about a bright future for the stock market just the day before was now replaced by negativity and dampened enthusiasm,' and further notes that 'the statement of the left leaders made the investors and intermediaries' hearts sink in despair.'[3]

We were in a crisis. On the one hand, action had to be taken immediately, and India as a country had to demonstrate that it had strong risk management systems in place. On the other hand, those in authority had lost the election and felt that they had no moral right to take any policy decision or even make any statement. The situation was further complicated when the SEBI chairman decided to leave the country on Saturday to attend a four-day international conference in Jordan. He was accompanied by whole-time member T.M. Nagarajan and another official. SEBI was left with only one whole-time member—A.K. Batra in Mumbai.

We were worried about what would happen on Monday, 17 May, when the markets would reopen. We were getting constant feedback from investors, fund managers, bankers and market participants about growing negative sentiment. We made inquiries from stock exchanges, who were in constant touch with brokers and custodians. There was fear in the market. There was a build-up of 'sale' orders and hardly any 'buy' positions. The foreign investors were panicking. Domestic investors such as LIC and SBI, among other banks and mutual funds, were watching the developments with confusion and had reached out to us too.

The media was raising genuine but disturbing issues, and there was nobody in authority whom they could quote—neither the PM, finance minister nor chairman of SEBI. The finance secretary and I decided that I should visit Mumbai and be there on Monday when the market reopened. I talked to many SEBI officials, stock exchange officials, intermediaries and large investors. They all admitted that there was nothing wrong with the economy and the market had no reason to be panicky in theory, but there was nobody to provide the required comfort or assurance.

When dealing with periods of extreme volatility, SEBI rules prescribed that if there was a market-wide impact, and the general index (Sensex or Nifty) fell by more than 10 per cent from the closing of the previous day (Friday, 14 May, in this case), trading would be suspended for one hour. If after one hour of reopening, the index fell further by 5 per cent, the market would be shut for the next two hours. If it dipped further by 5 per cent, the market would be closed for the rest of the day.

On 'Black Monday', 17 May, I was in Mumbai when the first 10 per cent dip took place within seconds. This triggered the circuit filter to shut the markets for one hour. When they reopened, the market dipped fast and the second circuit filter came into effect within seconds. This was an unprecedented event for the Indian market.

We used the next two hours to gauge the mood and provide as much comfort as possible. There was fear that if the market reopened after the mandatory two-hour 'calming' period, it would fall again drastically and cause the market to shut again. The negative sentiment would spill over to the next day. The looming question was whether or not the market should be declared closed for the rest of the day. But that would be a big setback and send the message that the well-laid-out risk management measures had failed. There were suggestions that established rules had to be overlooked. We were in constant touch with the finance secretary and other officials, and they were in touch with Bajpai in Jordan. Questions were being asked by the media about what SEBI was doing and where the chairman was. In his book Bajpai writes that on Monday morning his wife called him in Jordan from India asking, 'Where are you? Everyone is accusing you of having run away?'[4]

Bajpai decided to skip the conference in Jordan and rushed back on the first available flight. Meanwhile, information trickled in that some institutional investors had started placing 'buy' orders. It was decided by SEBI and stock exchange officials, with the support of the finance ministry, that the rules should be followed. Forced closure of the market through the bypassing of established rules would only add to the panic. When the market reopened after two hours of shutdown, some 'buy' orders had already come in. Some domestic investors felt that it was a good opportunity for them to buy at the lower prices and make profit. There was also relief that the rules would be followed, and the government was not panicking. The market recovered a bit and trading took place normally for the rest of the day.

Although I was in Mumbai and in regular touch with SEBI officials throughout the day, I avoided visiting the SEBI office during the trading hours. This would have given a misleading signal to the media that the government was taking extraordinary measures in the absence of the SEBI chairman during the crisis. As soon as the market closed, I visited SEBI. The officials were debating whether to address the press or not. The media was eager to receive some communication from SEBI. A press briefing did take place, where the media was told how rules had been followed and that stock exchanges had a fail-safe mechanism built in so that there was no crisis regarding settlement of trades on that day. They were also comforted by the fact that trades executed on previous days and trades which were due for settlement on Monday had gone off smoothly. There was no default and no cause for worry. From the next day, things settled down, and the market was back to normal.

During my long career in public service, I have seen several crises. I have faced serious law and order situations, handled communal riots and extremist violence, and dealt with earthquakes and floods. Through all this, what I have learnt is that nothing aggravates a situation like leadership vacuum, which was the case in this situation, and turns it into what Bajpai rightly describes in his book as a 'tsunami'.

4

CMD, UTI AMC

I joined as chairman and managing director (CMD) of UTI AMC in the last week of October 2005. The organization had been without a chairman for almost a year, after Damodaran had left it for IDBI. One of my first tasks was to get the board reconstituted. Anita Ramachandran, a famous expert on human resources (HR), joined the board. So did Prithvi Haldea, S.H. Bhojani, Hemant Bhargava and P.R. Khanna. This brought in a very healthy mix of experts in the areas of HR, capital market, law and accounting.

Something had to be done immediately to arrest the falling market share. The assets under management at the beginning of the financial year 2005-06 had come down to as low as Rs 20,000 crore from about Rs 65,000 crore at the time when the organization had not been bifurcated into SUUTI and UTI AMC. UTI agents, who had been the key distributors across households all over the country for more than three decades, had switched over to selling schemes of other mutual funds. Some of them had become agents of LIC.

To revive sales and galvanize the entire sales force, a new scheme was introduced. With a lot of effort and planning, UTI was able to mobilize in a new fund offer (NFO) amounts in the range of Rs 300 crore to Rs 500 crore. This fund could mobilize

Rs 1800 crore, which was a large number by all accounts. The entire organization was involved. Very detailed planning was done and hundreds of meetings were held with distributors and advisors across the country. A massive communication strategy was designed and launched. This fund restored the prestige of the organization.

The market noticed the renewed vigour in UTI. However, this short-term achievement had to be matched by long-term changes and deep-rooted reforms. An external consultant was brought on board, and an exercise was conducted to reimagine the role and vision of UTI. Instead of importing knowledge and wisdom entirely from outside, the approach was to have a large number of employees at all levels be seriously engaged in the exercise to create our vision. This helped motivate the work force as well.

The recommendations were implemented swiftly. The research and fund management department was overhauled, and the marketing department completely restructured. New verticals were created. A new HR policy was introduced. The policy of a performance-linked bonus, which was introduced by Damodaran in a limited way, was expanded. The employees could now receive as high as 150 per cent of their basic pay as a bonus. Additionally, an employee stock options plan was introduced. This was unheard of in an organization owned by PSUs. The scheme was designed such that 100 per cent of UTI employees got stock options.

The new changes also sought to improve the experience for the client. At that point, UTI's client service mechanism was very poor. If somebody had invested in two different schemes of UTI, they had to get two separate statements of accounts, and a consolidated snapshot was not available. Rehauling this entire mechanism took months, but consolidating operations of all the schemes was taken up and completed on a war footing.

More than inducting new leadership, the greater challenging task was how to deal with senior employees who refused to change their thinking and were still rooted in the old mindset of monopolistic and protected functioning. While most of the employees showed willingness to adapt as per new thinking to meet the challenges, there were some who had to be dealt with differently. The UTI board made an objective assessment of their performance. The JPC had identified some senior employees who were definitely involved in the earlier decisions taken at UTI that were without merit, and perhaps guided by extraneous considerations. We had the unpleasant task of dismissing some senior executives, including executive directors, from service. Another set of employees were those not involved in any irregularity, but who were not at all aligned with the strategy to deal with the new challenges. The board asked me to deal with these identified executives. All of them were well-intentioned and committed to the organization, but they refused to look at issues from a fresh angle and realize that change was needed. About a dozen senior executives were asked to leave UTI. To this day, the conversations that I had haunt me. It is not easy to tell an employee who has worked for a company for many years that their services are no longer required. At a personal level, it was a very, very difficult conversation. To be fair to them, most of them decided to quit gracefully. Nobody threatened to resist or challenge the decision. Most of them parted with dignity. The board and the employees reposed complete faith in me.

Micro Pension Scheme

UTI launched some innovative schemes that received tremendous trust and support, and helped enhance its reputation. It launched the micro pension scheme in partnership with the Self Employed Women's Association (SEWA) of Ahmedabad. Fifty thousand women, who had no regular source of income, joined the scheme by saving as little as Rs 100 per month for their old-age income security. Ela Bhatt, Renana Jhabvala and Jayshree Vyas formed the top leadership at SEWA, and worked hard to make this scheme a success. From UTI, Jaideep Bhattacharya, the head of marketing, and Amandeep Chopra, the fund manager, piloted the scheme successfully. It was not very easy for the executives of a mutual fund to convince the women living in a slum in Ahmedabad, who hadn't had exposure to formal education or stable jobs, about the need for old-age income security. But they made sure the messaging was right, and encouraged the women to save for their future. Chidambaram, who came to inaugurate the launch in Ahmedabad, called it the 'beginning of a pension movement in the country'. The success of this scheme led to its being tried out in Bihar for milk farmers.

The Bihar State Milk Co-operative Federation runs a successful dairy operation. Its brand Sudha is very popular in the eastern part of the country for its dairy products. Amir Subhani, its dynamic managing director, had taken a lot of interest in the project under the guidance of Chief Minister Nitish Kumar. When the scheme was launched, 50,000 milk farmers joined. Nitish Kumar handed over the first cheque of Rs 64 lakh, which was the joint contribution of the farmers, some of them paying even Rs 100. The scheme was tailored to the milk farmers and had the innovative mechanism of deducting a small amount (with the consent of the farmers) from the fortnightly payment for the milk they had supplied, and pooling it for investment. Care was taken that each individual had their own retirement account and could easily check the balance at any time. This scheme contributed significantly to UTI's popularity in Bihar.

When the government of Bihar started taking welfare measures for the benefit of the girl child, UTI launched another scheme Mukhya Mantri Kanya Suraksha Yojana, where the state government provided Rs 2000 per girl child upon her birth, which could be invested in the UTI scheme and be returned to the girl child with the dividend when she turned eighteen. Hundreds of thousands of girls across the state were enrolled under this scheme.

Under UTI, we also created a new company to manage pension funds called UTI Retirement Solutions Ltd in December 2007. It was 100 per cent owned by UTI AMC, and a new board was created for the company. The new CEO and other staff were brought in from UTI. Research and fund management was given priority. The bidding for business used to take place based on fees to be charged by the bidders. The company bid aggressively and was selected along with two others to get the business. It is a matter of added satisfaction to me that in May 2019 the total funds under management of this company exceeded the magic figure of Rs 1 lakh crore.

Hedging for Wheat Procurement by the Government of India

India has been a net importer of several important products, such as petroleum, foodgrains, agricultural products, and metals. The prices of these products in the global markets are determined in the derivatives market. Huge commodity or financial firms dominate these markets, but none of these markets exist in India. Metals are traded in London, petroleum products in New York or Singapore, and wheat in Chicago. Neither the Government of India, its agencies such as Oil and Natural Gas Corporation (ONGC), State Trading Corporation of India Ltd (STC), Food Corporation of India (FCI), nor even any private players from India are active in these markets. India is a significant buyer of these products, but we are left at the mercy of international trades so far as price discovery is concerned. During my stint in the Capital Markets division, I had pointed out this lacuna, and made a proposal that the country should develop the expertise of hedging against the prices of these products. In 2007, I was appointed to head a committee to assist and advise the government in using the overseas wheat derivatives markets for access to the required quantities of wheat. The committee included Susan Thomas from Indira Gandhi Institute of Developmental Research and Bharat Ramaswami from Indian Statistical Institute.

It was a very educative exercise. We negotiated with some of the largest traders in the grain market, examined various alternative modes and studied the global markets intensively. We had to update the Empowered Group of Ministers (EGoM) headed by Pranab Mukherjee from time to time. The committee examined various alternatives, such as call option with physical delivery, exchange-traded options, exchange-traded futures, among others. After evaluating all the options, we arrived at the conclusion that the preferred option for the government would be to opt for an auction contract. If not feasible, feature contracts were also permissible.

Being a completely new area, the committee first developed the evaluation criteria for bids. We decided on the criterion of lowest implied volatility. Besides the constantly changing wheat prices, the changing freight costs also had to be taken into account. We closely tracked both the options and futures markets. Going by the trends, we decided to go with the futures route. As a result of the committee's effort, a profit of USD 32 million was made over a period of one year.

While this was a one-time experiment, it is important that the country develops sufficient capabilities and systems so that it can automatically hedge in the future procurements of foodgrains, pulses, petroleum products, metals and other high-value items. Unfortunately, this has not happened so far.

Long-term Solutions for UTI

While the short-term and medium-term solutions had been planned and implemented, we were also worried about the long-term solutions. The idea to invite SBI, LIC, BoB and PNB to be the shareholders was taken in 2003 in the context of providing comfort to the larger investment community so that the capital market sentiments were not disturbed. However, since these organizations had their own mutual funds, this could only be a temporary arrangement. While operations proceeded smoothly, the ownership issue still had to be sorted out.

My first thought was to ask UTI Bank (now Axis Bank) to be the sponsor and owner of UTI. There had been examples of banks promoting their own mutual funds. Importantly, UTI Bank also did not have its own mutual fund at that time. I broached the idea with P.J. Nayak, the CMD of UTI Bank. He was in favour of it but was not sure whether I would be able to get the approval from the government and all the shareholders without any hassle. Earlier, he had had a bad experience in dealing with SUUTI and the government. The RBI had proposed that the post of managing director in private sector banks should be separated from the chairman of the board. As per the articles of UTI Bank, SUUTI had a right to nominate the chairman and three other directors, as well as a controlling stake in UTI Bank. SUUTI chose to implement this change at UTI Bank, at a time when the RBI had not yet mandated it or made it compulsory. A resolution was moved by SUUTI at the UTI Bank meeting that the post of chairman and managing director should be separated. The manner in which it was done was a big affront to Nayak. He took it up with the finance minister and others in the government. Chidambaram was furious at this decision taken without government permission or even without a discussion among the board of SUUTI. Eventually, the decision had to be reversed, and Nayak remained CMD for several years thereafter. However, this incident had scarred him, and he was convinced that he wanted to deal less and less with the government or government-related entities.

I pointed out to Nayak that a merger between UTI and UTI Bank would have the further advantage of UTI Bank being able to retain the brand name as the brand ownership was with UTI AMC. In spite of all these favourable factors, Nayak was reluctant to take a chance. Instead, he decided to change the brand name, and UTI Bank became Axis Bank. The merger of UTI AMC with UTI Bank did not proceed any further.

IPO of UTI AMC

As the first option had not worked out, the next logical step was to attempt a broad-based ownership by getting the company listed on the stock exchange. UTI would become the first in the country to do so. Approvals from shareholders and the government were obtained smoothly in 2007 and 2008, and papers were filed with SEBI for the initial public offering (IPO). The employees fully supported the move. After a series of discussions with SEBI, we received approval, the 'final observation letter'. However, by June 2008, the winds of the global financial crisis had started blowing. The Indian market was also being severely affected. Investment bankers, who had had a very positive view about the expected price, now marked it down by as much as 25 per cent. They advised against the IPO, citing that it was the wrong time to do so. Considering all the factors, the idea of the IPO had to be dropped. Market conditions remained shaky for the next three years, and the IPO was shelved. It was only much later that other asset management companies such as Reliance AMC, ICICI AMC and HDFC AMC would get listed.

With the tie-up with UTI Bank ruled out and the IPO plan shelved, we turned to the other option of taking on a strategic partner. A number of potential partners were sounded out, and confidential dialogues were initiated. Finally, T. Rowe Price, a large US asset management company, agreed to buy a 26 per cent stake in UTI AMC. Then came the extremely difficult task of concluding negotiations with the buyer, obtaining approvals from shareholders and the regulatory authorities, and formalizing the partnership. Imtaiyazur Rahman, Debashish Mohanty and Satish Dikshit provided excellent support in concluding the deal. Nobody could imagine that UTI AMC could pull off a tie-up with such a large US institution. An important advantage of the deal was perceived to be that T. Rowe Price could help upgrade the skills of UTI AMC's research and fund management teams. UTI AMC could benefit from their system-based investment approach. It was also expected that some of their global or regional funds that were investing in India could be routed through UTI AMC. Unfortunately, not all the anticipated benefits of this deal were realized. T. Rowe Price hardly allocated any money for investment in the schemes of UTI AMC, but they did contribute to the training and skills upgradation of the UTI AMC staff. One reason for this could be that after I left UTI AMC in February 2011 to join as the chairman of SEBI, the process of appointing my successor got mired in controversies and was delayed for years. Until today, T. Rowe Price is still a 26 per cent shareholder. But other anticipated benefits from such a large and globally renowned investor are yet to be seen.

Years later, in 2013, when as chairman of SEBI, I attended a function to celebrate the tenth year celebration of the new UTI, Finance Minister Chidambaram was present. In my speech at the time I mentioned that SEBI was not comfortable with the current shareholding pattern as all the four initial sponsors had their own mutual funds and this was against the spirit of the mutual funds regulations. However, nothing came of it. Later, SEBI amended the regulations so that no institution could hold more than 10 per cent of shareholding of more than five mutual funds at the same time. A period of one year was given to implement this, but LIC, SBI, BoB and PNB have still not done so. The shareholding issue is holding back the realization of the full potential of the talent residing within UTI AMC.

PART II

Joining SEBI, Initial Challenges and Market Development

5

The Regulatory Architecture

Among the present-day regulators in the financial sector in the country, the RBI was the first to come into existence, in 1935. All others came up post–Independence. There is a major difference between the regulators created in the early years after Independence and those created post 1991 reforms. The idea behind the first kind was to provide legislative backup to the government so that it could regulate specific sectors of commerce and business. Laws on regulating the commodity derivatives markets, stock exchanges, or raising capital from the public are examples of this kind. But the regulatory institutions remained housed within the government. Some government official was notified under the provisions of these Acts to discharge the functions of the regulator. Either there were no appellate provisions or, if there were any, the appeal was to be presented before another officer of the government. For example, statutory authorities had been created under the Forward Contracts (Regulation) Act or the Securities Contracts (Regulation) Act, but these authorities/institutions functioned more like subordinate or attached offices of the ministries. While performing these statutory tasks, they worked directly under the control and superintendence of the government and were not independent.

Post liberalization and economic reforms, various services earlier reserved for or dominated by the public sector were also opened up to the private sector. In such a situation, objectivity demanded that the supervision and regulation rested with an independent authority removed from the government. This was needed to avoid a perception of conflict of interest between the regulatory function of the government and the ownership function of a commercial organization. As the global economy became increasingly linked, it also became important that a regulator with sectoral expertise be instituted. This structure was needed even more to provide confidence to foreign players if they were to be welcomed into the country.

SEBI became the first such authority to be so created. The need for SEBI was articulated by the government in the budget speech of 1988, and it was created thereafter through an executive order. But because of fear of parting with the jurisdiction of the government and a turf war between different arms of the government, a statutory SEBI could not be created until 1992. It required a Harshad Mehta scam to generate the momentum for the enactment of the SEBI Act. The government was at pains to create a positive impression about the actions it had taken post the Harshad Mehta scam. Eventually, the ordinance route was taken to create an independent SEBI rather than wait for a detailed process of lawmaking in the Parliament. This instance was not an outlier, and instead a pattern has emerged since. Whenever a crisis has developed in the market, changes have taken place in the Act first empowering SEBI through the ordinance route, and formal Parliament approvals have taken place only later. Between 1992 and 2017, the SEBI Act has been amended multiple times through ordinance and very few times through the normal legislation routes.

Appointment of the SEBI Chairman

Many people feel that the Vastu of SEBI is defective. Being dragged into controversies is in its DNA. It started with the selection of its second chairman, G.V. Ramakrishna (G.V.R. to many). He became the first chairman to function under the newly enacted SEBI Act. Other bureaucrats and he himself felt that because he could not be accommodated as a secretary in the Government of India in a ministry that he deserved, he was shunted to SEBI in Mumbai, an organization that was not yet fully functional. When SEBI came into existence in 1988, the first chairman was S.A. Dave. G.V.R. was appointed in 1990 at a time when there was no certainty when the SEBI Act would be passed. The stock exchanges did not want SEBI. The brokers did not like it as they had to pay fees to SEBI out of their own revenue. Several court battles later, which were settled in the Supreme Court, brokers agreed to pay fees to SEBI.

G.V.R.'s tenure saw the foundation for a solid institution being laid. He was a well-meaning person with vast knowledge of the government and public institutions. Public interest was uppermost in his mind in all situations. He was succeeded by D.R. Mehta, another respected person who had worked in the ministry of finance as well as in the RBI as a deputy governor. But in all these appointments, the question that remained unanswered was whether the government was selecting somebody out of expediency or actual suitability for the job. There was no consistency about the tenure of the chairman, and different people were selected for different lengths of time. A search-cum-selection committee was created. But who would be the members of the selection committee and who would be heading it was always left to the discretion of the finance minister. This left the impression that there was no objective and consistent criterion being followed.

Mehta was replaced by Bajpai. When the three-year tenure of Bajpai was about to end in early 2005, the search-cum-selection committee was headed by C. Rangarajan, and had, among others, members such as Rakesh Mohan in the committee. Interestingly, this committee considered many names, including that of Damodaran, but recommended that Bajpai should be given an extension of two years. When the proposal went to the Appointments Committee of the Cabinet (ACC), there was a change of heart at higher levels. The same search-cum-selection committee met again and modified its earlier recommendations in favour of Damodaran instead of Bajpai, and this decision was approved by the government. Damodaran joined in February 2005.

The Selection Process of 2008

The process becomes more controversial in 2008. An episode of manipulating the IPO process by some unscrupulous elements had come to light in 2005. Multiple applications under fictitious names and often having the same address were processed by the depository participants of NSDL and Central Depository Services Ltd (CDSL). SEBI arrived at the decision that there were serious lapses on the part of NSDL in handling the IPOs.

An enforcement action against NSDL by SEBI was going on at the same time that the chairman of SEBI was to be selected. Damodaran himself was keen to receive an extension. Chidambaram, as finance minister, had decided that in order to remove the perception of arbitrariness from the selection process, the setting up of the search-cum-selection committee should be institutionalized within the rules framed under the SEBI Act. As a result, a rule was framed about appointing a search-cum-selection committee with the Cabinet Secretary as its head.

This was a very wise move, and this concept of selection through a committee under the cabinet secretary has now been extended to appointments in all regulatory bodies in the financial sector. The rule also provided that the chairman of SEBI could be appointed for a period up to three years and was eligible for another term subject to the overall limit of sixty-five years of age.

The committee invited applications. Since it was a search-cum-selection committee, it was possible that in addition to those who had applied for the post, the committee, in its wisdom, could directly invite other suitable candidates for interaction and consideration. Damodaran was not prepared to apply for a second term for a post that he had already held for three years. He and a few others were invited for an interaction with the committee. He refused to attend the interaction but wrote a long letter highlighting what all had been his achievements as chairman of SEBI. I did not apply for the post. However, I was invited by the committee, along with another candidate. The other candidate met the committee and told them that in view of a regulatory action underway against NSDL, which he was heading, it would not be fair for the committee to consider him until the matter was resolved by SEBI. After interacting with all the candidates, the committee recommended two names in order of preference (i) U.K. Sinha and (ii) Jaimini Bhagwati. However, the government in its wisdom decided to appoint another candidate instead of either of the candidates recommended by the search-cum-selection committee. It was peculiar that in its communication to the ministry of finance about the decision of the ACC, a detailed note was sent from the PMO saying how Damodaran had done a good job and he ought to have been given an extension. But in view of the objections of the finance minister, the PM approved the appointment of another candidate.

This was quite an unusual situation. The views of the PM are normally recorded in the files of the PMO. Only the final decision is communicated to the ministries in brief. Here, quite unexpectedly, the full notes of the PM were communicated to the ACC and the ministry of finance. What was the anguish in the minds of the PM behind this selection is still a mystery.

Problems inside the SEBI Board

The days of rushing to the Supreme Court through public interest litigations (PILs) against senior level appointments had not yet arrived. Neither Damodaran nor I approached any court or sought any redressal from the government regarding the appointment of the new chairman. Matters regarding the IPO scam were still underway at SEBI, where the new chairman's role as head of NSDL was also under examination. Hastily, a letter was issued by the government specifying a special procedure to handle the NSDL matter. Normally, a whole-time member or the chairman conducts a quasi-judicial hearing, but in this case it was provided that this matter should be heard by a committee of SEBI board members, from which the new chairman should recuse himself. A committee under G. Mohan Gopal, an independent member of the SEBI board; V. Leeladhar, deputy governor of the RBI; Anurag Goel, secretary, ministry of corporate affairs—all members of the SEBI board—was formed for this purpose. For unforeseen reasons, Goel could not participate in the proceedings and only Gopal and Leeladhar dealt with the matter. Unfortunately for the new chairman, the committee in its findings made scathing observations about the role of NSDL. When this report was placed before the SEBI board, it observed that the committee had exceeded its brief and gone beyond the terms of reference for which it was set up. As such, its findings were non est (non-existent) under law. Under the SEBI Act, the only agency that can hear an appeal against an order passed by a whole-time member of SEBI, an adjudicating officer of SEBI or the SEBI board is SAT. But, in this case, a two-member SEBI board finding was declared non est by the SEBI board itself. Gopal protested against this decision, but he was overruled. He was an eminent jurist and wrote letters to the PM. He also filed a PIL and narrated how one whole-time member of SEBI had harangued and harassed him.

The Selection Process of 2011

In 2010, when the process for the new SEBI chairman began, Pranab Mukherjee was the finance minister. There had been an avoidable public controversy between SEBI and Insurance Regulatory and Development Authority (IRDA) about the jurisdiction over insurance companies offering unit-linked insurance products (ULIPs). SEBI was right in holding that if a product is substantially an investment product and a very small portion of the amount invested is going towards buying insurance cover, then it should be regulated by SEBI and not IRDA. But IRDA did not want any involvement from SEBI in the matter.

The issue could not be resolved by the High Level Coordination Committee (HLCC) consisting of the Governor of the RBI, SEBI chairman, IRDA chairman, PFRDA chairman and secretary of DEA. It finally reached the finance minister. He advised the two regulators to sort it out amicably, and if they could not, they should seek clarity from a judicial authority such as a high court or the Supreme Court. Mukherjee became upset when, in spite of his sound advice, SEBI sent legal notices to insurance companies for the alleged violation of the SEBI Act. An ordinance was issued by the government creating a statutory

Financial Stability and Development Council (FSDC). One of the provisions of this ordinance was that in case of disputes between two regulators, the judgement of the finance minister as chairman of FSDC would be final.

When this matter was being debated in the Parliament, Mukherjee made the famous comment asking what could the public expect from the government when two regulators were fighting like 'petulant children'. It was in this context that the process of selecting a new chairman began towards the end of 2010. I was invited for an interaction with the committee headed by the cabinet secretary. The SEBI Rules (pertaining to the appointment of the chairman and a whole-time member) had by then been amended. The rules provided for a term for the chairman and whole-time member of up to five years, a revision from the previous provision of up to three years. This change had taken place in 2010. One of the questions before the government was whether the rules should be applied retrospectively and to the existing chairman. The proposal to grant him another two years was approved by the finance minister and sent to the ACC for their approval. It was widely expected that the proposal would be approved and thereafter the same precedence would apply to the two whole-time members K.M. Abraham and M.S. Sahoo, who were also completing their three-year tenure in the middle of 2011.

But the ministry of finance recalled the extension proposal from the ACC and decided to advertise for the post of a new chairman. It is widely believed that the main reason for this decision had been the development regarding the row between SEBI and IRDA on ULIP. Another embarrassment for the government was the controversy around the NSDL matter and how SEBI had been handling it.

Gopal had raised this matter with the prime minister conveying his strong disapproval of the functioning of the SEBI board and also written articles in the press. A case filed by him questioning the jurisdiction of the SEBI board in exonerating the chairman of SEBI and NSDL by holding the findings of the committee non est is still pending in the Supreme Court. The retired chief justice of India J.S. Verma also wrote an article in the media supporting Gopal's stand and commenting on the state of affairs in SEBI at that time.

My Initial Years at SEBI

The interview for the post of chairman of SEBI took place in December 2010. That same evening, I got a call informing me that the committee had unanimously recommended my name for selection as the chairman. While I was hoping to be appointed this time and for the revised tenure of five years, to my surprise, the appointment order stated that I was to take the post 'initially for a period of 3 years . . .' In spite of this setback, I joined SEBI in February 2011. One of the first major challenges that I immediately faced was to take a stand before the Supreme Court in the PIL filed by Mohan Gopal in the C.B. Bhave–NSDL matter. This matter had been placed before the SEBI board. It was felt that the earlier stand of refusing to relook at the matter would be an affront to the Supreme Court since it had specifically asked the views of the SEBI board under its new chairman. A decision was taken to inform the Supreme Court that the case would be re-evaluated. When the matter was heard by SEBI, an order was passed against NSDL. The latter then appealed before the SAT, which set aside the SEBI order. SEBI has gone to the Supreme Court against this order and until the time of this writing, the matter is still pending. Immediately after the decision was taken by the SEBI board to relook at the matter against NSDL, a series of very strong attacks, against me in particular and SEBI in general, were initiated.

For the first three months after joining SEBI, I did everything to learn about the inner workings of the organization. I tried to understand the issues, had a series of internal meetings, and met market participants and other experts so as to draw up a strategy and vision for SEBI. In May 2011, I had a very big town hall meeting with officials at various levels. It was a fairly long conversation trying to identify the role of and current expectations from SEBI, the strength and weaknesses of the organization, the path it needed to take and how it should go about it. I unfolded my plan about what I wanted to focus on and what I expected from the team. As is customary, a summary was presented by one of the whole-time members after this talk. He was effusive in his praise for my understanding, knowledge and vision about SEBI and the securities market. He also made a remark that he was unlucky that his tenure would be coming to an end shortly and he would not be there to implement this vision.

But within two to three weeks of this meeting, the same person wrote a letter to the prime minister making allegations against the finance minister and his Officer of Special Duty (OSD) Omita Paul, and also drew me into the controversy by saying I am not able to withstand pressure from the minister and his team about helping a few business houses, which he named in the letter. The letter got leaked in the media and sparked off serious discussions across the country.

When the existing chairman was denied a two-year extension and the selection process for a new chairman was initiated, it became clear that this person was not likely to be granted another term as a whole-time member. He then approached the chairman to appoint him as the director of National Institute of Securities Markets (NISM), Navi Mumbai. NISM had been created by SEBI to be a nodal centre for studies and research in securities market. It has a board of governors headed by the chairman of SEBI. The proposal was approved by the chairman of the board of governors of NISM, i.e. the SEBI chairman. However, the process also required a separate approval from the chairman of SEBI, although they were one and the same person. For some reason, may be because of the controversy that had already surfaced, the chairman did not back up his own recommendation. He rang me up to say that since my notification as chairman of SEBI had been issued by the government and I was about to join shortly, he would like to record in the file that he had discussed the matter with me and that I had no objection to the appointment of the whole-time member as the director of NISM. I advised the exisiting chairman that it would not be proper because until I had assumed my duties I had no locus standi in SEBI. He should function as the SEBI chairman with full authority until his last day in office and take decisions that he thought were right. The chairman recorded in the file that the matter should be placed before his successor and did not approve the appointment.

When I came to SEBI, the whole-time member approached me to approve his NISM appointment so that he could stay on in Mumbai. However, I found that the board of governors of NISM had erred in not following the procedure of appointment of the director. The rules also required that a set of names should be recommended by NISM, so that SEBI could select one of them. But only one name had been sent to SEBI in this case. No reason had been recorded as to why the procedure prescribed under the rules had not been followed.

The whole-time member was naturally disappointed with me. Another reason I didn't want to bypass the rules was that there were allegations of misuse of power and influence related to a property purchased by this person in Mumbai. The government sent a communication asking for SEBI's views. I got the matter examined by the Chief Vigilance Officer (CVO), and she found that there was no evidence of any irregularity in the purchase of the property. A report with these findings was sent with my approval to the government. But the government did not close the matter and kept on sending many supplementary queries. I did not want to appoint this member as director of NISM bypassing rules, especially when a vigilance matter against him was still pending in the government.

I suspect that all these matters put together must have weighed on his mind when he decided to write that letter to the PM, dragging me into the controversy. One day he informed me in a very agitated manner that some income tax officers had also visited his home and his income tax filing was being scrutinized. He believed that there was a conspiracy against him, and was feeling harassed. This could have been the immediate provocation for the letter he wrote. His tenure ended on July 2011, within five months of my joining.

Public Interest Litigations

The first PIL challenging my appointment was filed in September 2011. While writs of quo warranto challenging appointments in public offices are not rare, I have the single distinction to date of five PILs being filed against me one after another in the Supreme Court. By the grace of God, and the independence and fair play of the higher judiciary, all these PILs were eventually dismissed, and I stood vindicated. In some cases, the petitions were filed on behalf of people with very good reputations, people who have been crusaders for good governance, fair play and transparency. The five PILS are a testament to the kind of groundwork that would have been done to convince a retired lieutenant general of the army, a retired DG of police and a celebrated police officer, and a retired IAS officer that something sinister was taking place in the ministry of finance under Mukherjee and that SEBI was being compromised under my leadership.

A person who lives in the same housing society as the retired DGP ran into him one day and asked him whether he knew me or SEBI. He confided that somebody from his cadre had painted a very dark picture of the minister and the organization, and this had led him to append his signature in the list of petitioners. The retired IAS officer knew me very well. He was abroad when the petition was filed on behalf of the organization he belonged to. He called me to say that he was not aware of the circumstances and that he held nothing against me.

When the first PIL was dismissed, a second one was filed quickly. Fortunately, this too was dismissed. Everything remained quiet for some time. Work at SEBI continued smoothly, and a number of important reforms were taken up. Many important enforcement orders were passed. All of this must have upset some people. Then a third PIL was filed before the Supreme Court against my appointment. This time, more research had been conducted about my present and past life. Voluminous material had been gathered, and a very detailed petition was filed.

The petitioner was a person who had introduced himself as a PIL activist. He had never met me, or cared to check facts with me. He seems to have filed more than 100 applications under Right to Information (RTI) to obtain details about my past postings, the circumstances in which I was appointed to UTI AMC or the situation under which I left it to join SEBI. The thrust of his petition was that not only was my appointment to SEBI wrong but also the earlier one to UTI AMC. I had allegedly suppressed material facts from the government and there was a conspiracy between me and two successive finance ministers—P. Chidambaram and Pranab Mukherjee. Senior-level appointments such as those of chairman of SEBI require approval from the Appointments Committee of the Cabinet (ACC). ACC rules require, inter alia, that a detailed form that has to be filled by the joint secretary of the administrative ministry and sent to thc ACC secretariat. An argument was made in the PIL that since all the columns in this form had not been filled, I was responsible for it and hence unfit for the post! I am sure the petitioner was not ignorant and deliberately listed this as a reason, even though he must have realized that a future appointee has no information about which forms are being filled by the administrative ministry while sending a proposal to ACC and whether it is being done correctly.

As PILs have evolved in the last decades, these have come to stay in the political and judicial system of the country. Even the members of the higher judiciary realize that it is prone to abuse and misuse. Universally, PILs are recognized as a powerful and inevitable tool to provide justice in cases where the affected people are so poor or marginalized that they cannot approach the courts. A PIL can also be filed to spur the government from inaction when a large number of people are affected or to generally keep a check on the executives where equity and fair play are endangered. It goes to the credit of the judicial system in the country that except for some examples where the orders cannot be justified, the judiciary has shown a significant amount of restraint, public-spiritedness and wisdom in dealing with such matters.

The hundreds of RTI applications filed and material gathered for the third PIL against me must have cost a lot of time and energy, and the litigations a lot of money. Some of the biggest and most expensive lawyers in the country were engaged. Even if it is granted that they all worked pro bono without charging any professional fees, it must have required a very high degree of persuasion on the part of the petitioner to convince so many legal luminaries to devote their time and energy for a matter projected to be of grave public importance.

The Supreme Court saw through the game. After giving enough opportunities to both parties of the case, the Supreme Court remarked in its final judgment that the petitioner had failed to meet the strict criteria of uberrimae fidei (utmost good faith). It observed in its judgment that 'the proposition (of my influencing the decision-making process) is so absurd that the allegations with regard to mala fide could have been thrown out at the threshold'. The court also noted, 'It is a well known fact that in recent times SEBI has been active in pursuing a number of cause célèbre against some powerful business houses.' In its order the Supreme Court also made some strong comments about the petitioner and the whole-time members. Some of these comments were expunged later when prayers were made to that effect.

The persistence and perseverance with which these cases were pursued was really alarming. A practice has emerged that when a PIL is likely to come up, a series of articles in the media are generated. Judges are, after all, human beings and they read the same newspapers and watch the same TV channels. The trick is to malign a person through the media.

A large number of complaints and letters were written to various authorities. In one case, a letter was written to the Central Vigilance Commission (CVC), and an article appeared in the media stating that the CVC was examining the complaints. The entire letter was narrated in the article. The idea was to repeat the same thing which was before the court through media articles to create a negative bias. Another ploy practised while filing PILs is to take advantage of the position that the contents of a petition filed or arguments made before the court can be reported. An enterprising subeditor can write a catchy headline giving the impression that points made are actually the findings of the court rather than the allegations made by petitioners. My family and I went through an agonizing time facing many such articles and attacks. At the same time, SEBI employees were confused and demotivated, but they continued to perform their task with unabated zeal.

While the letter written by the whole-time member to the prime minster had no connection with the PILs—as maintained by the petitioners—all the petitions before the court had this letter as an annexure. It is a matter of great satisfaction to me and to other public servants that the Supreme Court came down heavily on the person who wrote that letter. The court held, 'We are unable to take the allegations made by Dr Abraham seriously, as the same seems to have been actuated by ulterior motive.' It also said, 'It is manifest that the letter written by Dr Abraham was clearly motivated and espouses no public interest.'[1] A very trying period came to an end on 1 November 2013 when the Supreme Court finally delivered the order. But days before the order was delivered, there was a last-ditch effort to misrepresent facts and malign me in the media, so as to again create doubt in the minds of the judges. The same petitioner who had filed the PIL had shot off dozens of complaints to government authorities. One was regarding alleged irregularities in granting approval for a stock exchange by SEBI. It goes to the credit of the system of checks and balances prevailing in the media that a mail was received by SEBI, asking for our comments on the proposed write-up. The facts were that this decision had been taken three years before I came to SEBI and it was taken in spite of advice from the ministry of finance then available on the records of SEBI that the group proposing to open the exchange was not 'fit and proper' under law. I contacted the editor of that business newspaper and apprised him of the facts. Convinced about the truth, he ensured that the article would not paint a dark picture, and the true sequence of events about the stock exchange licence was published.

After the judgment was delivered by the Supreme Court, the petitioner as well as the erstwhile whole-time member filed a petition for review to expunge some of the remarks against them in the judgment. A very senior lawyer, who has been the law minister earlier and who rarely appears in the courts nowadays, had to personally appear in the court to represent the petitioner. The court, while agreeing to expunge some of the remarks against the petitioner, held that the remarks against the whole-time member would not be expunged. It held that those remarks were required to explain why the court had come to its findings. However, it clarified that these remarks would not be used in any departmental action against the whole-time member.

Applications under RTI

The matter did not end there. The design to malign me was so intricate that the same person filed an appeal before the chief information commissioner based on the same facts that the Supreme Court had reviewed and provided a decision on. The appeal was ultimately rejected. Thereafter, two more PILs were filed in the Supreme Court on different grounds. These too were rejected.

But the question that remains unanswered until today is about the forces driving these attempts. The Supreme Court has thrown some light in its judgment, but the rest remains a mystery. What needs to be kept in mind is that SEBI takes decisions as an institution and not as an individual. SEBI is a vital regulator, and it has to remain ever vigilant and often perform unpleasant tasks. If its officers hesitate in performing their duties due to fear of harassment, it can lead to disastrous consequences. In the larger context it is important to create an objective environment in which public servants can perform their task without fear in the light of the responsibility given to them, rather than worry about motivated complaints to authorities, recourse to PILs, and getting maligned in the media. Of course, a transparent accountability mechanism must be ensured in these vital institutions. I will go into this in more detail later in the book.

6

Mutual Funds

One of the first set of issues that required my attention when I joined SEBI was the mutual fund industry. It was declining in size, and for months the outflow of funds had been higher than the inflows. Questions were being raised about the future of this industry. The UTI crisis of 2001 had shaken the whole mutual fund industry. It took years before mutual funds started gaining the confidence of investors and began growing again. But a decision taken by SEBI in 2009 dealt another blow to the industry, from which it was still recovering when I joined.

This issue was regarding entry load. If, for example, Rs 100 was invested in a scheme, Rs 2 would be adjusted towards entry load, and only Rs 98 would be invested in the account of the investor. In a way it was the fees charged for entering a mutual fund scheme. Other costs, such as management fee, fees for brokers and registrars, etc., were further charged from the Rs 98 in the investee's accounts. Of course, a ceiling for total expense ratio was prescribed by SEBI. The competitiveness of mutual funds placed the distributors in a demanding position. Many unhealthy practices had developed, much against the interests of investors. They were advised to exit one scheme and invest in another, known as the 'churning' of portfolios, not because it was in their best interests but because distributors earned extra commissions from each such transaction. The suitability of a scheme from the aspect of the risk profile of an investor was hardly considered. Instead, distributors recommended whichever fund house gave them higher commission. SEBI had been expressing its disapproval over such unhealthy practices for quite some time, but the mutual fund industry was unable to come together and make concerted efforts to curtail the malpractices. In 2009, SEBI put a ban on entry load in one major decision.

When I came to SEBI in February 2011, there was an expectation that I would reverse the decision on entry load taken by my predecessor. As chairman of Association of Mutual Funds in India (AMFI), I had criticized the SEBI decision at that time. But my objection was not to the decision per se but the manner in which it was implemented, without giving any opportunity for the mutual fund industry or distributors to prepare for it. In the UK, a similar move took three years to be implemented after the consultation papers were floated. In India, it was implemented in less than two months.

After taking up my post at SEBI, I realized that reversing this decision, that too after two years of its implementation, would be a retrograde step not in the best interests of investors. It would also be against the consensus emerging in other parts of the world about curtailing costs and fees, and reducing the dominance of distributors. It was decided that a comprehensive review of the issues facing mutual funds would be undertaken. Wider consultations were conducted with all the stakeholders. It was kept in mind that while measures were required for the growth of the industry, the ultimate focus had to be to promote and safeguard the interests of investors.

We discovered that the reach of the industry was not deep; 85 per cent of the assets were from the top fifteen cities. Measures were required to increase penetration beyond major cities. In the same scheme of a mutual fund there were different plans for small and big investors. Bigger investors bore lower costs and charges. Even if someone invested directly, without the help of an advisor, the costs were the same. In addition to the ceiling on the expense ratio, there were separate sub-ceilings on fees for different costs, which brought rigidities. There was a need to expand the cadre of distributors, and also to set up a mechanism to alert a small investor about the risks involved with different schemes. Creating awareness among investors was also important.

SEBI undertook a series of measures. In order to incentivize the industry to reach out to customers in smaller towns, an extra commission of up to thirty basis points (0.30 per cent) was allowed. In helping small investors fill in mutual fund application forms, an extra Rs 100 to Rs 150 could be levied. The sub-ceilings on total expense ratio were removed. A new cadre of distribution was created, and the costs of direct plans were reduced. Product labelling in different colours was mandated so that an investor could easily gauge the risks involved. Differential cost structures in a scheme were done away with. It also became mandatory for mutual funds to set apart two basis points (0.02 per cent) of their income for investor education. The industry had the option to pool this money and launch national campaigns.

Provisions were made for consolidated account statements for investors. Mutual funds became the first industry in the entire financial sector where a monthly statement could be obtained across different schemes of multiple funds. This provided more comfort as well as control to ordinary people over their investments. Today, it is possible to get one consolidated picture of all investments—mutual funds as well as other securities.

At the same time, mutual funds were asked to be more transparent and uniform in disclosing the performance of their schemes. SEBI started calling CEOs and fund managers for a discussion if a scheme consistently recorded bad performance. Senior officials of mutual funds were asked to disclose their remuneration on websites.

All these measures led to a substantial increase in the size of the industry. From a total size of less than Rs 7 lakh crores in March 2011, the industry touched nearly Rs 25 lakh crores in March 2019.[1] What is more satisfying is that instead of being largely a manager of short-term and liquid funds, the industry has been able to attract more long-term equity money from different corners of the country. A large number of people have now developed the habit of investing small amounts of money month after month through systematic investment plans (SIPs). The industry has undergone a major change, and is now also playing a significant role of being a counterbalance to flows from foreign portfolio investors.

In 2014, the *Economic Times* conferred the Business Reformer of the Year award to me for my work as chairman of SEBI. The jury acknowledged how SEBI had cracked down on pyramid schemes, cleaned up the IPO market, and managed to regain retail investors. They appreciated how SEBI's insightful thinking had helped revive the mutual fund industry. The jury acknowledged that the inclusive approach had not only improved SEBI's efficacy and investor confidence but also accorded it with the distinction of being a regulatory body of global standards. In 2015, CNBC-TV18 conferred the India Business Leader Award to SEBI for 'outstanding contribution to the cause of Indian business'.

7

The Corporate Bond Market

Besides equity, corporates also need to raise debt from the market. A vibrant debt market helps reduce the dependence on banks, creates an alternative source of funds, and helps lower costs. For the investor, the advantage is that bond prices are transparently known so that they can decide when to exit and at what price. SEBI, the RBI and the government have been continuously trying to help the bond market grow. A number of measures were taken to simplify the process of issuance and bring uniformity to the system. For example, earlier, even if a company had its shares listed on the exchanges and information about its affairs were continuously disclosed to the public, rules required that such a company had to disclose all this information all over again in a separate format to raise debt. This process was done away with. SEBI also ensured that information about bonds issued through private placement was also reported to the stock exchanges so that the larger market was aware of it. Secondary trading on bonds was also facilitated on stock exchanges. Rules regarding credit rating agencies were made stronger and uniformity was implemented in the rating symbols. At the same time, rules about debenture trusts were tightened. Since credit rating agencies and debenture trustees are also supervised by SEBI, better coordination amongst different players in the chain could be established. The government also helped by allowing pension funds to invest in corporate bonds. All these measures together led to substantial growth in the corporate bond market.

The Municipal Bond Regulation

One of the most important initiatives of SEBI was to formulate regulations for municipal bonds. Municipal bodies are quasi-government entities that have received a constitutional position and recognition after the Seventy-fourth Amendment of the Constitution. Their major sources of revenue are property tax, professional tax, user charges, assigned revenues from stamp duty, grants in aids and subsidized funds from the government. They can also borrow from funding agencies as well as from the market. However, bonds raised by municipal bodies in the past have been mainly on the strength of the guarantees provided by the state governments. In 1988, Ahmedabad Municipal Corporation issued the first municipal bond without any government guarantee. It was able to raise Rs 100 crore. Other municipal bodies have also attempted raising money from the market, but the total amount raised from the domestic capital market through taxable bonds has been less than Rs 500 crore.

SEBI undertook the task of utilizing the capital market infrastructure to help municipal bodies raise capital. In 2015, it published its municipal bonds regulations, which provided a framework for issuance and listing of bonds. At the same time, it provided for disclosure of information that could help potential investors. Municipal bodies in the country own valuable properties in almost all towns and cities of the country. They take up projects for water supply, sewage treatment, transportation, and developing markets and buildings. Investor protection required that the funds raised should not be comingled with the general accounts of these bodies. It was, hence, provided that the money raised had to be kept in a separate escrow account, and could be used only for the purpose for which the money had been raised. The projects had to be income-generating and self-sustaining so that from the income of the project the bond-holders could be paid and there was no dependence on the general finances of the municipal bodies. The ministry of urban development was very supportive of these revised rules. Until the end of March 2019, eight municipal bonds under these regulations have been issued and close to Rs 1400 crore has been raised by Greater Hyderabad Municipal Corporation (GHMC), Pune Municipal Corporation (PMC), Indore Municipal Corporation (IMC) and Bhopal Municipal Corporation (BMC).[1]

For the development of this market, a substantial amount of training and capacity building, improvement in account keeping and management and awareness building is required. Going by the success of municipal bonds in developed markets, this route can be an important source for raising capital in the future.

8

Foreign Portfolio Investors

Developing a policy on allowing foreign investments in India has been a difficult one. After economic reforms, the policy on investment from abroad was liberalized. The two broad categories of investments are:

i. Foreign direct investment (FDI), where a foreign investor invests in an Indian company with an intention to participate in its management and its affairs. The accepted threshold for FDI is an investment of 10 per cent or more in the shares of the company, subject to limits prescribed by the government for different sectors like banking, media, civil aviation, etc.
ii. Foreign portfolio investment (FPI), where a foreign investor can invest upto 10 per cent in a company, with no intention of managing its affairs. These are financial investors expecting to make a gain from the performance of these companies.

The subject of foreign portfolio investment came to be handled by SEBI within the overall parameters of FEMA. SEBI Foreign Institutional Investors (FII) Regulations, 1995, were formulated for non-residents who were otherwise fit and proper to make an investment into the country. An FII had to be registered with SEBI, and was allowed to have sub-accounts. In the early years, there was a worry that FIIs are volatile as they invest in hordes and abandon the market at the first sign of a problem. The second and more important worry has been that of holders of participatory notes (PNs). An FII registered with SEBI mobilizes money from non-residents. But these non-residents might exit from these positions and sell their investment outside India to a third person. This did not require any approval from any Indian authority, nor was any record of the new buyer captured in SEBI's system. This person gets a participatory note from the FII as proof of his participation in the underlying investment in the Indian company. The worry in India has been that neither SEBI nor any other body used to have any information about the PN holders. FIIs were not obliged to share the information with SEBI. It also opened up the possibility for residents of India to use this opaque structure of PNs and FIIs to buy shares in Indian companies for which they may not be otherwise eligible. During the Ketan Parekh scam, it was discovered that some Indian corporates and operators in the market took their ill-gotten wealth out of the country and used the same money to invest in companies through the PN route, thereby manipulating the market.

This has been a cause of concern for the government, the RBI, SEBI as well as tax authorities. Frequent discussions were conducted to check this practice. Over the course of my career, I have been involved in this matter through various responsibilities that I have performed. In 2004, while working in the ministry of finance, I was a member of the committee headed by Dr A.K. Lahiri to make recommendations for changes in the FII regulations.

In 2009, while I was working as the chairman of UTI AMC, the ministry of finance set up a working group under my chairmanship to review the existing policy on foreign inflows by portfolio investors, non-resident Indians (NRIs) and foreign venture capital funds. The group was tasked with identifying the challenges of meeting the financial needs of the Indian economy through foreign investment. Under the FII Regulations, 1995, the process of registration as a FII was difficult and time-consuming. Investors faced multiple difficulties as they had to often deal with contradictory and complex rules for different categories of investors. This led to a lack of transparency and also created opportunities for regulatory arbitrage, i.e. one group of investors benefitting over another group.

The working group felt that the current regime, while prescribing different rules and obligations, did not provide the mechanism to capture all the details of the real investors. It felt that the rules had to be simplified, keeping in mind that the know your client (KYC) details of the investors were appropriately captured. The consensus among the group was that the standard for KYC should be at par with the best standard in the world. But beyond this, there should not be any discrimination between domestic and foreign investors. The group examined data for periods when due to global or domestic factors, there had been wide-scale volatility. We found that contrary to belief, there was no unidirectional behaviour. During volatile times while many sold their stake, there were others who bought more, thinking of the developments as a buying opportunity. The net position was not large. The conclusion that emerged was that the more diversity is built in, the more overall behaviour will cancel out, and the impact on the market will be minimal. The working group recommended that there should be one single window for the registration and clearance of portfolio investment regulations, which does not distinguish between investor classes. We called it qualified foreign investors (QFI). As a result, FIIs, foreign venture capital investors (FVCIs) and NRIs could be abolished as investor classes. The responsibilities for the registration and KYC processes could be given to reputed large global firms that themselves function as regulated entities. The group also was of the view that in order to remove uncertainties around what is an FDI and what constitutes a portfolio investment it should be clarified that investment below 10 per cent of the shares in a company should be considered as an FPI and above this as an FDI. An important piece of advice from the group was that in sectors where there was a ceiling on FDI, the QFI investment ceiling should be counted in the same manner that an Indian mutual fund or insurance company is counted. FDI and FPI should not be clubbed for testing the prescribed ceiling.

The report by the working group was submitted in July 2010. It was very well received by experts, the media as well as the government. SEBI made several changes in its regulations in the light of these recommendations.

That the PN route can be misused had again been brought to the notice of SEBI in 2008 when the Financial Conduct Authority (FCA), the counterpart of SEBI in the UK, passed on information about this route being abused through complex structures in countries across Europe and in Mauritius to bypass regulations. A large foreign bank had been the facilitator and a very large business group in the country the perpetrator. Finally, in early 2011, the case resulted in a settlement with SEBI, of an amount of Rs 50 crore. It generated a lot of public debate about how this route was being misused and the market was being manipulated.

SEBI began tightening the norms from 2011. One of the first measures we took was to ensure that the details of the PN holders had to be shared with SEBI whenever required. There was a serious pushback from various large foreign banks and custodians, but SEBI stood its ground. Several other measures in reporting and capturing data were also implemented. We wanted to tackle the issue at the root cause, which propelled even genuine investors to take the PN route. The main reason behind avoiding registering as an FII or its sub-account with SEBI was considered to be the procedural hassle. It used to take months, and was costly and not helpful when an investor wanted to take advantage of a short-term opportunity. By the time the formalities got completed, the opportunity could have already been gone. We decided to have a complete review of the regulation. A committee was set up, headed by the former cabinet secretary K.M. Chandrasekhar, and it provided some innovative solutions. FPIs were brought into three categories:

i. Foreign governments and their agencies, central banks, sovereign wealth funds, etc.
ii. Well diversified funds, banks, pension funds, university endowments, etc.
iii. All the rest

The KYC requirements were made very simple for the first two categories as the risk involved in those cases was much lower. The need for direct registration with SEBI was done away with. Large banks or custodians were given the authority to register an FPI on behalf of SEBI. But the most important revision was that only category-1 and category-2 FPIs were authorized to issue PNs. Category-3 FPIs, such as individuals, corporates or hedge funds, could not issue or buy PNs. Our approach was two-fold: (i) to make investment easy for high-quality investors and (ii) to plug all loopholes to avoid misuse. While there is need to maintain vigil and continue to make further improvements, it is heartening to note that the size of PNs which was in the range of 50 per cent in 2012-13 fell to 3.4 per cent of the total outstanding values of FPIs in the country by end of 2017-18. In 2018-19, it further reduced to 2.3 per cent.

On the other hand, India has become a significant market for FPIs. There have been years when FPIs in the country have been far greater than those in China. The cumulative net investment of FPI at the end of 2017-18 was more than USD 250 billion.

9

Alternative Investment Funds

Globally, start-ups, new generation companies and other smaller companies depend on a class of investors different from mutual funds or insurance companies for funding. Alternative investment funds (AIFs) raise money from different sources, and take the responsibility of investing in private companies that are unknown and untested. These funds have to take a call on the future growth potential of these investee companies, remain invested for a longer period, and often end up providing operational and marketing support to these assisted companies. While technological advancement and entrepreneurship in India have progressed steadily, in SEBI we discovered that unlike other parts of the world, the environment to support investment in these companies was lacking.

A SEBI venture fund regulation had been in existence since 2000, but the domestic pool of money was not easily available to the venture funds. Banks, insurance companies and pension funds were reluctant to support entrepreneurs. At the time, angel investing had not picked up. Setting up a foreign venture fund was not helpful as there were strict limitations on sectors where these funds could invest. Often foreign funds used to commit funds through a circuitous process and by following a FDI route.

SEBI decided to resolve the issues by formulating an AIF Regulation in 2012. In order to address the concerns of the RBI and the government, three categories were prescribed. AIF category I consisted of the venture funds and other socially useful funds. Category II were private equity funds. Both of these categories were not permitted to borrow. Category III were hedge funds and others. Favourable tax treatment was given by the government to category I and II funds. Angel funds were also envisaged. In 2016, AIFs invested more than USD 16 billion in different companies. In 2018-19, the total funds invested were close to USD 32 billion. Now, even corporates and rich individuals are setting up funds to invest in start-ups. Many of them are also mentoring the assisted companies, besides making financial investments.

In 2015, SEBI set up a committee under N.R. Narayana Murthy to suggest further improvements in the AIF space. SEBI has implemented a majority of these recommendations. Today, the combination of technological innovations, entrepreneurship and AIF have brought India to a position where the ecosystem is comparable with the best in the world.

10

Investor Education and Awareness

The level of financial literacy in the country is abysmally low. Incidents of unauthorized fund collection where millions of gullible investors suffered highlighted the need for SEBI to accelerate its initiatives. The ministry of corporate affairs has an investor protection and education fund. As per the provisions of the Companies Act, dividends from companies that go unclaimed for more than seven years are credited to this fund. The fund is a non-lapsable one, i.e. it is not part of the general funds of the Government of India and can accumulate year on year. The RBI too has its own funds for this purpose. But it was discovered that minimal activities had been taken to educate investors.

SEBI had instituted a programme for conducting financial education through resource persons, which could be teachers, lecturers or other qualified persons in various parts of the country. NISM of SEBI conducted a training programme for them, designing a new curriculum, at SEBI's cost. These people were then given the task of conducting these programmes in their own areas, which included schools, colleges, and professional groups such as bar associations and medical associations. The entire cost of resource persons was borne by SEBI.

After what had happened with Rose Valley Group, Saradha Realty India Ltd (SRIL) and Sahara, a massive push was given for this programme. We revitalized this programme, strengthened the training and expanded the activities. More than 4000 people were empanelled and trained all over India. More than 50,000 workshops were conducted, with close to 40 lakh participants in nearly 550 districts in the country over 2012–16. The programmes were conducted in local languages so that the beneficiaries could understand the contents. Apart from this, another programme targeting students was launched in the secondary-level institutions across the country.

It was felt that besides investor education programmes targeted at selected individuals, awareness through TV, radio, print and other means of mass media was also required. A large-scale campaign was launched with SEBI's own funds to caution investors against unregistered or unauthorized money-collection schemes. The aim of this messaging was also to let people know how to approach SEBI in case of any grievances. The campaigns were carried out in Hindi, English and eleven major regional languages. A digital media campaign added to the efforts to alert and educate investors. In addition, campaigns were launched in collaboration with AMFI and used the efforts of external experts. A committee under K.V. Kamath was empowered to approve the campaign and its launch. A national programme of financial literacy in coordination with all the regulators was also launched. These played a big role in alerting ordinary citizens across the country to be cautious about their rights as investors and whom to approach in case of complaints.

The Harvard Business School (HBS) conducted a case study on SEBI in 2016. It was for the first time that HBS had done a case study on any regulator. The paper recognized the achievements of SEBI in the past six years and its contributions to international policy developments. The case study dealt with how strict action was taken against entities such as SRIL, Sahara and PACL, and how SEBI managed to hold its ground even during times of extreme adversity. The case study highlighted SEBI's corporate governance initiatives, revision of insider trading regulations, and measures to revitalize the mutual fund industry. The authors also acknowledged the investor education initiatives of SEBI.

11

REITs and InvITs Regulations

Even after the successful completion of a real estate project, the developer or other investors in the project remain locked in for years together as outright sale is often not possible. The problem is more acute in commercial real estate, such as office buildings or malls. The general practice is to rent out these buildings on lease so that the developer has a regular revenue inflow through rental income. In such cases, the money invested cannot be released for taking up more projects. In developed markets such as Singapore, Japan, the USA and Australia, the mechanism of a business trust has been found to be very successful in unlocking the investments. A business trust is created, and the shares of the company that has developed the property are transferred to this trust. It can receive investments from pension funds, insurance companies or other long-term investors. The developer gets value in lieu of the shares transferred to the trusts. By this mechanism, completed projects that are revenue-generating can attract long-term investors. The money released can be utilized to take up new projects. Most landmark office buildings, malls and other commercial buildings all over the world have been developed through this mechanism. The real estate industry in India did not have the benefit of this option until 2015 as the market had no provision for this sort of regulation.

SEBI embarked on an exercise to provide a mechanism for real estate investment trusts (REITs) so that investors as well as developers had a clear set of rules guiding them. There was intensive consultation with experts, market functionaries and the government to formulate these rules. During the discussion, the idea came up that infrastructure projects built on a public–private partnership (PPP) model could also be covered by similar regulations, but unlike real estate projects where the developer had ownership of the land and building, the operator (concessionaire) in an infrastructure project did not own the infrastructure. A road, port or airport continues to be owned by the government or its authorities. The concessionaire only has the right to operate or manage the project for a definite period, after which the infrastructure assets revert to the government agency. Thus, instead of a single regulation, two separate regulations were drafted: (i) REITs Regulations and (ii) Infrastructure Investment Trusts (InvITs) Regulations. The regulations were well-received by the investor community, and foreign funds too showed interest. The advantage was that the regulations applied to projects that had already been executed. As such, the risks involved with projects in the construction phase were eliminated. Since the projects were revenue-generating, pension funds and other long-term investors expecting a steady income found the scheme attractive.

However, several tax-related issues needed to be clarified. Finance Minister Arun Jaitley was very supportive of the initiative, and over the next three budgets, these issues were resolved. For example, when shares of the company owning the project are transferred for units of the business trusts, there should not be any long-term capital gains tax. This was accepted by the government. When the question arose about the applicability of minimum alternate tax (MAT), it was clarified that the same would not apply. Exemption was granted from dividend distribution tax when the business trust distributed dividends to its investors. With these clarifications, the India regime became comparable with the best in the world.

By March 2019, four InvITs registered with SEBI have raised more than Rs 11,000 crore. One REIT has also been able to raise close to Rs 5000 crore.

PART III

Regulatory Reforms

12

Primary Markets

The primary market is the mechanism through which companies can raise capital while selling their securities. Securities include debt or equity or a combination of the two. Primary markets serve a prominent purpose in the economy of a country anywhere in the world. If the financial services industry is fairly developed, these are important sources of money that can be invested in these companies. These are, for example, insurance companies, pension funds, mutual funds, banks, companies with surplus funds, wealthy individuals, family offices and last but, not the least, small investors. In the early years after Independence, the government had to be extra careful to ensure that the scarce capital was allocated in a manner that best served the policies of the government. The other imperative was to provide protection to small investors. Controller of Capital Issues (CCI) was empowered to approve (or disapprove) the raising of capital through the primary market. CCI had the authority to decide when a company would be permitted to raise capital, what should be the price of the individual shares and the total amount that the company could raise at a time. The merit or the quality of a share was decided by CCI, and market forces had no mechanism to discover the price of a share when it was issued.

When SEBI was created, it took over the responsibilities of CCI. It marked a major shift in policy. Going by international practices, SEBI introduced a system where all relevant information had to be disclosed by the company to the public so that they could take a call on whether or not to buy a share and the price at which it should be bought. From a merit-based approach, the country moved towards a disclosure-based approach. In the nineties, SEBI was new and still evolving, and relatively inexperienced. Unlike the developed market, India did not have enough expert and knowledgeable investors, such as mutual funds and insurance companies, which could value the shares of companies properly. Used to the earlier CCI rules, the public also took time to understand the new approach. Many companies took advantage of the shortcomings of the system. They provided misleading and incomplete information, created hype around their shares in the media and raised capital from the public. It was later discovered that many of these companies did not have business operations and some of them were even difficult to trace. As the surveillance mechanism was still evolving, the price could also be manipulated after listing. Many of these issues in the mid-nineties therefore tanked and many people lost money. It was a major setback for reforms in the market.

Learning from these episodes encouraged SEBI to strengthen the process. The disclosure requirements were made more elaborate. SEBI had to strike the right balance between protecting the interests of investors on the one hand and not imposing obligations that were too onerous and unaligned with the rest of the world on companies.

Listing Gain

In 1977, there was a change in policy on FDI. Foreign companies were mandated to have domestic shareholdings as well. Some like Coca-Cola and IBM left the country because of this new requirement. Many others decided to stay on. They had to divest their holdings by issuing a portion of ownership to domestic investors. This was also the time when the prices of shares were determined by CCI. Most of the time, the price fixed by CCI was much lower than the intrinsic value the company commanded. Those who were successful in the allotment of these shares in the IPO became rich overnight, because on the day of the listing of the shares, the value increased sharply, leading to significant profits. A tendency of 'gain on the listing day' became prominent in the psyche of Indian investors and continued for decades. It continued even under SEBI's disclosure-based system. Some smart investors, often with the help of merchant bankers and brokers, gamed the system by taking advantage of the asymmetry of information. They invested not for the long-term but to sell shares on the day of listing at a hefty gain, mostly at the cost of the ordinary retail investor.

This issue of 'listing gain' was tackled in 2016 by introducing the system of 'call auction in the pre-open market on the opening day'. Earlier, a share could go up by 100 per cent or more on the opening day and then decline by a large higher percentage—all on the same day. This created confusion and often investors would watch helplessly. Now, the price discovery takes place in the pre-open market. This becomes the reference price for the day and the movement remains within a range prescribed by stock exchanges and SEBI.

IPO Process

While prescribing rules for the IPO, SEBI has to be mindful about protecting the interests of investors. This was more important in the context of several incidents in the past wherein unscrupulous promoters with fictitious or non-existent companies had raised money through IPOs and disappeared. Therefore, SEBI had to prescribe criteria for the eligibility of companies which can raise money from the public.

While prescribing the eligibility of a company for listing, SEBI had to specify some basic criteria of the business turnover of the company or their profitability track records. The question arose that there may be some companies that may not be profitable but displayed strong potential to grow fast. Special rules had to be made for these types of companies. The entire IPO process involved holding road shows, sending application forms to different parts of the country, collecting the applications and cheques within a given period, reconciling the accounts, making the share allocations and refunding the money received through cheques. All these processes took a long time. A large number of intermediaries were involved across the country, including merchant bankers, registrar and transfer agents, bankers to the issues, brokers, sub-brokers and custodians. Until 2009, the process would take months. The investors either did not receive their shares in time or the refund of money in their bank accounts in time. Dematerialization of shares, of course, helped. In 2009, SEBI conceived a quicker way to complete the primary market process by Application Supported by Blocked Accounts (ASBA). Under this mechanism, a cheque did not have to be issued to apply for buying shares, and the bank accounts did not have to be debited. Only a lien was recorded in the bank accounts of the applicants. Once the IPO was closed, bank accounts were debited only to the extent of the value of the number of shares allotted and not up to the entire amount applied for. This saved the hassle of refunds. The added advantage was that the customer continued to earn interest on the money in his account.

Besides the amounts lying blocked in the bank accounts of the applicants, the other major drawback was that if the process took an unusually long amount of time, the applicant was exposed to change in the share price during the period. Through the new measures that were introduced, the period of applying to an IPO was gradually reduced from twenty-one days to twelve days. This period was further reduced from to six days in 2016. The process involved coordination between hundreds of banks and their branches, the RBI, individual banks and investor associations.

Taking advantage of the disclosure-based regime, many companies priced their securities much higher than the company actually deserved. Merchant bankers were also party to that. Between 2010 and 2014, in almost two-thirds of the IPOs, the actual trading price was far below the listing price. This meant that the investors were losing money from the day of allotment of shares. Naturally, this reduced their interest in the primary market. Questions were raised about what SEBI was doing and how effective its supervision was.

SEBI introduced the concept of due diligence record of merchant bankers in 2012. It also prescribed that along with information about the company, the track record of the merchant bankers must be disclosed prominently in the offer documents. Initially, there was resistance, but later, merchant bankers discovered that more stringent SEBI rules were actually empowering them and helped add credibility and repute to the merchant banking industry. A merchant banker, for example, had to disclose how many of the IPOs undertaken by him during the last three years were trading below the issue price. For the first time, merchant bankers started posing difficult questions to companies. This in turn helped modify corporate behaviour, ushering in structural, logical and user-friendly information about the companies, comparison among peer groups and more transparency.

The reforms in the primary market in the last ten years have brought India into a league of countries with the most robust systems in the world. During 2017-18, more than Rs 1,05,000 crore of equity was raised from the primary market. In fact, in 2016-17 and 2017-18 the total quantum of capital raised through the market (debt and equity) was more than the net growth in bank credit.

13

Secondary Markets

Whenever benchmark indices such as Sensex and Nifty fall by a few percentage points on any day, there is a sense of gloom that spreads across the country. It leads to media reports on how investors have lost lakhs of crores of rupees in value. Similarly, when indices jump substantially on a day, there is euphoria. Stock exchanges are thus regarded as the barometer of the health of an economy and indicators of the sophistication of its financial markets. While there may be multiple factors behind movement in the market, if prices fall, invariably the instinct is to suspect failure of governance of the stock exchanges and the regulator SEBI. This feeling is accentuated by the incidents of market misconduct and scams in the past, where the exchange administration and SEBI have been found wanting.

Stock exchanges provide the platform where the trading takes place. But their role is much greater. If a person has paid money to buy shares, or another person has offered shares for sale, then on the appointed day (T+2, two working days after the trading) the buyer must get the shares they paid for and the seller must get the money for the shares they sold. Ensuring this 'settlement of trade' is the paramount duty of the stock exchange. Failure of settlement in any market is counted as more serious than the failure of a bank. As such, SEBI prescribes strong rules for risk management, settlement guarantee and governance of the exchanges. Governance of stock exchanges and clearing corporations requires the focused attention of SEBI. Knowing the perils of a single monopolistic exchange in a country of the size of India, the stated objective of SEBI and the government was to encourage competition amongst stock exchanges. It was thought risky to encourage monopolies in such a critical area for the financial sector. SEBI has to ensure that all exchanges are treated equally and no one institution receives an unfair advantage. In the past, controversies have often arisen in granting permission to a stock exchange to trade in a new product or incentivizing growth of business. There was a controversy regarding grant of licence to MCX-SX (now Metropolitan Stock Exchange) for trading newer products, and regarding following the ownership structure as prescribed by SEBI. The decision by NSE not to charge any fees for currency derivatives trading had created a serious situation for BSE and MCX-SX. Ultimately, the Competition Commission of India had to pass an adverse order against NSE and impose a penalty on it.

The Bimal Jalan Committee had made recommendations in 2010 about the governance and ownership of stock exchanges. In 2012, we in SEBI decided to formulate the Stock Exchanges and Clearing Corporations Regulations (SECCR), incorporating many of the suggestions of the Jalan Committee. A few recommendations of the Jalan Committee that were not accepted were linked to capping profits of exchanges and whether to allow these to be listed. SEBI felt that capping the profit of a business by its regulator was not a forward-looking idea. But, SEBI also had to ensure that in the drive towards reckless profiteering the settlement and risk management functions of exchanges did not get compromised. As such, a high percentage of profit was earmarked through regulations for risk management and settlement guarantee. Similarly, strong safeguards were provided for listing of exchanges as well. These norms were uniformly applied to all the exchanges. Many regional stock exchanges (RSEs), which did not meet these criteria, had to be shut down, and suitable exit policies were formulated. All these measures have resulted in the cleaning up of the administration of exchanges.

The main focus behind all these revisions was to mitigate risk and take investor-friendly measures. Often there would be complaints from investors that brokers had conducted trades on their behalf but without their authentication. Brokers would obtain a power of attorney from clients and trade based on the same. Often, disputes arose between brokers and their clients. To counter this, SEBI prescribed that at the end of the trading day, SMS or e-mail alerts would be sent to clients so that they were made aware at the earliest about trades undertaken on their behalf. At the same time, the mechanism for the redressal of disputes between clients and brokers was strengthened, and the number of centres for arbitration in the country were increased.

Surveillance: SEBI had created a sophisticated surveillance mechanism immediately after the Ketan Parekh episodes. This was further improved with data warehousing facilities. Past data and trends were checked and evaluated without any delay. The system generated alerts whenever there were suspicious or irregular transactions, such as circular trading or insider trading. Many enforcement cases were initiated by SEBI based on these surveillance inputs. It is a matter of great satisfaction that no major market misconduct has taken place in the last decade or longer.

Misuse of Stock Exchanges for Tax Evasion

The surveillance system in SEBI discovered that one important motive for manipulation is the desire to evade paying taxes.

With the introduction of the computerised screen-based trading, anonymous orders had become possible. The buyer or seller could be located in any part of the country. It was no longer possible either for the seller or the buyer to know who was trading at the other leg of the transaction. The computer did the matching of trade. With this, audit trail became possible. Everybody thought that the irregularities in the old open-outcry system would be put to a stop. However, unscrupulous operators had devised methods to misuse the new system for evasion of tax.

Some of the methods being followed in misusing the stock exchange system for tax evasion included:

(i) Client Code Modification
(ii) Misuse of capital gain tax regime

I. Client Code Modification

Throughout the trading hours on a trading day, thousands of brokers across the country keep punching millions of 'buy' and 'sell' order on their computer screens. Since the order-book visible on the screen keeps changing very fast, it is possible that while punching an order a broker might genuinely punch the wrong code of the client on whose behalf the buy or sell orders were to be placed. Understanding this difficulty, SEBI and the stock exchanges provided that at the end of the trading hours half an hour extra time should be given to the brokers to rectify these mistakes and modify the client codes every day. The misuse which became prevalent was that if a client did not make any losses during a particular day and he still wanted to reduce his tax liability he would record some bogus trading losses through modification of client codes. Of course, this required connivance of the brokers. If, on the other hand, there was a person who had not made any gains that day and had made losses, he had no tax liability. Through the mechanism of client code modification, the second person would wrongly 'transfer' his losses as if the orders had been punched on behalf of the first person. For committing this favour, the first person did not mind paying some amount of money to the second buyer through a cash transaction, of which audit trail was not possible. The number of client code modifications became so large that the estimated value exceeded Rs 56,000 crore of trade very month. SEBI issued stern directions in 2011 to curb the practice. Details like the transaction ID, original client code, modified client code, PAN of both the clients, quantity, name, rate and value of the transactions were collected by SEBI and exchanges. Wide publicity of the new norms was given. Heavy penalties were also imposed. Stock exchanges were directed to conduct a special inspection and other disciplinary actions were also initiated. By October 2011 the client-code modification fell by 99 per cent to Rs 120 crore a month.

II. Claiming Bogus Long-term Capital Gains

A set of manipulators in combination with brokers was resorting to these practices. The idea was money laundering and to convert their unaccounted income in to a genuine one. Taking advantage of the 100 per cent exemption from long-term capital gains, these persons ended up not paying any tax whatsoever. A company which had very limited operations, and whose shares were rarely traded was identified. With the connivance of the promoter of that company an operator would be first allotted a big chunk of fresh shares through preferential allotment. Since the company had hardly got any operation or active number of shareholders, getting these approvals in company boards and general meeting of shareholders was not difficult. Over the next few months, share prices would be manipulated to rise by ensuring some very small volume of transactions at very high prices. Since the zero level of capital gains tax kicked in after twelve months, this practice could continue till then. After that the allottee of preferential shares (the operator) would exit completely by selling the shares at a higher price. The 'buyers' used to be its own cronies who had been paid cash as a commission for undertaking these favours. The motivation for such buyers was that their own money was not involved; they would be getting a commission and in due course they would sell the shares to book a loss. This loss could then be adjusted against their own profits to reduce the incidence of tax. Around 2014-15, a detailed survey was conducted by SEBI. Cases above a certain threshold of financial activity were taken up for detailed inspection. Inputs were also received from the Income Tax Department. After conducting these inspections, SEBI was able to take action in shares of close to 150 companies. Out of 290 entities against which action was initiated, 167 had been suspended. KYC analysis was done for more than 1800 entities. The action involved completing the investigation by ascertaining the true nature of the business of a company, transaction in its shares and the rapid pace with which the prices had moved. SEBI had to pass quasi-judicial orders against these companies banning them from participating in the market. All these cases were also sent to the Income Tax Department for necessary action at their end.

Platform for SME to Raise Money

SEBI has always made an effort to introduce new products and facilitate the raising of capital through new initiatives.

Facilitating small and medium enterprises (SMEs) to raise capital through stock exchanges in the same manner as large enterprises has been a long struggle for the government and the regulator, all over the country. Very few of them have succeeded. One of them is Nasdaq in the USA, which initially started as a platform for small-ticket information technology companies and later became a major stock exchange in the country. Other countries such as Brazil and Malaysia have also tried, but with limited success.

Efforts have been going on in India for long to help SMEs raise resources through the stock exchange. The primary rationale for the creation of regional stock exchanges, RSEs, was to help the local entrepreneurs enter the market. Small entrepreneurs have the disadvantage of their companies or products not being known across the country, with their clientele usually confined to a small region. It was thought that RSEs, where these entrepreneurs were operating, may bring companies and local investors together. In order to serve this purpose, a lower level of diligence and risk management practices were also permitted for these platforms. After the emergence of nationwide trading terminals in the mid-nineties, and corporatization and demutualization of stock exchanges, trading in the stock exchanges was confined to only BSE and NSE. This adversely affected the business model of RSEs. Furthermore, there was no compulsory listing of bigger corporations on these exchanges as they were hardly seeing any trading. Some intermediate steps were taken by allowing these exchanges to float a subsidiary that could become a broker registered with NSE and BSE, but this was also not very successful.

In 1999, a modern technology–enabled platform where SMEs could get listed was introduced through OTCEI. Another experiment was to create a separate platform called IndoNext on BSE in 2002. Both of them, however, did not take off. The main causes of failure were lack of sufficient interest from potential investors and lack of exit opportunities.

Efforts continued even later, but with limited success. Keeping these past endeavours in mind, in 2011, SEBI started working on another variant to help SMEs. A very fine balance had to be struck between creating incentives for companies and providing sufficient protection and safeguards to investors. Many conditions for listing, such as preparation of accounts, a minimum capital requirement, cost of compliance, size of the tangible assets of the company, etc., were diluted. At the same time, it was mandated that very small investors should be insulated from the risks of these platforms. The minimum investment amount was fixed at Rs 1 lakh. Compulsory underwriting and market-making were also mandated. These platforms met with modest success over the next eight years. Close to 500 companies have been listed on the SME platforms of BSE and NSE, and the total amount raised is more than Rs 6000 crore. The market capitalization has crossed Rs 30,000 crore.

However, this is only a small beginning, insufficient to meet the needs of capital-raising for the SME sector in the country. More needs to be done to help SMEs and start-ups raise equity and debt capital in a cost-effective and timely manner.

Merger of Forward Markets Commission (FMC)

Trading in commodities such as gold, silver, other metals, petroleum products and agricultural produce is regulated under multiple laws—both state and Central ones. State governments have more control over trade in agricultural goods. The ministry of consumer affairs is the nodal ministry at the Central level. To supervise forward-trading in commodities, the Parliament passed the Forward Contracts (Regulation) Act (FCRA). Forward Market Commission (FMC) was created under this act. But FMC was not fully empowered and had to seek various directions and approvals from the ministry of consumer affairs from time to time. As early as 2003-04, there was a recommendation by a committee headed by Wajahat Habibullah, the then secretary at the ministry of consumer affairs, that the functions of FMC should be passed on to SEBI. But that did not happen. The ministry made a different proposal to amend the FCRA and empower FMC, patterning it after SEBI. But neither decision could be taken for the next decade. Meanwhile, a serious episode took place in 2013 on National Spot Exchange Ltd (NSEL), which was under the supervision of FMC and the ministry of consumer affairs. But neither of them acted in time, and people lost Rs 5600 crore in trades on this exchange. There was huge uproar in the public and in the media. The government realized that FMC needed to be strengthened, along the same lines as SEBI. Realizing the synergy between SEBI's activities and the task of regulating the commodity derivatives market, the government decided to merge FMC with SEBI. While there are instances of one regulator spawning out of an existing one for undertaking some specialized responsibilities, such as National Housing Bank (NHB) or National Bank for Agriculture and Rural Development (NABARD) from the RBI, it was for the first time that two regulators were merged. There were separate rules for trading; the brokers had different outfits for commodities trading and securities trading; and the eligibility norms were different. After the merger, the commodities exchange and securities exchanges became universal exchanges dealing in both types of products. The process of the merger had to be planned very carefully as the exchanges were already functional, and no disruption in their activities could be allowed. The task was akin to two spacecraft docking in outer space. Elaborate preparations were made. Finance minister Jaitley played a pioneering role in getting the legal amendments passed in the Parliament. The merger of FMC with SEBI took place in September 2015 in his presence. The transition was designed in stages, to make sure it went off smoothly. In the first stage, the rules for brokers, trading and risk management were framed and implemented. The second stage saw activities for the development of the commodities market. It was a matter of big satisfaction for all of us in SEBI that the whole exercise went off smoothly, without any disruption.

14

Corporate Governance

In spite of measures taken by SEBI since the early 2000s, corporate governance was an area in need for urgent strengthening. Often there was doubt in the market about large shareholders or promoters carrying on transactions with related parties on terms that were not in the best interests of companies. Often, company assets or businesses were alienated in this manner. The roles of independent directors or audit committees of boards were not clearly delineated and social obligations of companies not clearly articulated. It was necessary to ensure protection of minority shareholders and other stakeholders.

In 2012, SEBI began by implementing provisions for minimum public shareholding in companies. The cause of mischief used to be the reality that other shareholders ended up having a small shareholding in comparison to promoters whose share used to be as high as 90 per cent to 95 per cent. This was against the rule of their being at 75 per cent or below. By following strict timelines, a majority of companies were compelled to reduce their shareholding. Companies that failed to meet the deadline were served with notices for legal action within twenty-four hours of the expiry of the timeline. This made clear to everyone that SEBI meant for its orders and policies to be taken seriously.

Earlier, the committee set up by SEBI and headed by Kumar Mangalam Birla had conducted its first major exercise to codify governance. This was implemented in 2000 by inserting a new clause in the listing agreement, i.e. Clause 49. Post-Enron and other episodes, when new challenges started appearing globally, another committee was set up by SEBI and headed by Narayana Murthy. It submitted its findings, based on which Clause 49 of the listing agreement was revised in 2003. This clause has both mandatory and voluntary provisions. These include promoting transparency in operations and reporting, protecting the rights of all shareholders and facilitating the exercising of those rights, and equitable treatment of all shareholders. Some principles were made mandatory and some voluntary. Some of the norms on the mandatory front included composition of the board with ample independent directors and the required procedure, creation of audit committees, their role and composition, quarterly report on corporate governance, annual compliance certificates, etc. The voluntary provisions included creating a remuneration committee of the board, a whistle-blower policy, etc.

The following decade did not witness significant changes, and in 2013, SEBI published a detailed discussion paper on governance. The Companies Act, 2013, also focused on corporate governance. Rules were strengthened further. For example, if the promoter of a company had pledged his shares with any financial institution, the same had to be disclosed. There was focus on transparency by putting all relevant information about the company on the website. SEBI also decided that the appointment of a CFO in a company or selection of the auditor should only be done with the approval of the audit committee. It also mandated electronic casting of the votes by shareholders. The voting percentage in companies shot up with this facility brought in place

The criteria for being selected as an independent director was made stricter. Often directors appointed by financial institutions or the government were counted as independent directors. SEBI took a call that a nominee director should not be considered independent as they were expected to serve the interests of the promoters or of nominating institutions. The ratio of independent and other directors was also regulated. The concept of limiting the number of directorships a board member could undertake was introduced, along with a maximum tenure for independent directors. It also became necessary for independent directors to give reasons for quitting the board. The role of the internal auditor was also emphasized and it was provided that the internal audit report should be sent directly to the audit committee. Other ideas included mandatory rotation of audit partners.

Remuneration of managerial staff is an important area from the corporate governance point of view. There may be a case where a company is making losses or not making a sufficient profit but the manager still receives disproportionate remuneration. This has to be controlled by shareholders, who are the ultimate owners. Voting requirements in such situations were made stricter so that minority shareholders could also have a meaningful say. SEBI also asked companies to disclose their voting patterns before the general public. Institutional investors like mutual funds were mandated to have a voting policy and also disclose the outcome of their voting. A certificate has to be given by auditors that compliance of all the requirements of governance norms have been satisfactorily met by the company. Non-submission or delayed submission of the certificates can itself invite adverse action. Compulsory whistle-blower mechanism was provided. The role of the audit committee was expanded. Independent directors were prohibited from getting a stock option. Once a year, a separate meeting of the independent directors was mandated. It was also mandated that at least one woman director be present on the board of top 500 companies. Social responsibility of corporates was also brought under focus.

In the hierarchy of lawmaking, enforceability of an agreement with the stock exchange stood low. In order to convey a stronger message about implementation, a new regulation called SEBI (Listing Obligations and Disclosure Requirements) Regulation, 2015 (LODR), was notified. One important aspect of LODR was that certain principles on corporate governance were enumerated in the regulation. The basic foundations of these principles are uniform information sharing, following the accounting standards, and furnishing timely and adequate information to stock exchanges so that the larger community is informed. It enumerated the right of shareholders to participate in decision-making, vote, ask questions, be safeguarded against abusive actions of controlling shareholders and have an adequate mechanism to redress their grievances. Equitable treatment of all shareholders was highlighted and the role of other stakeholders such as customers, employees and the community was also recognized. The landmark provision was that in case of any ambiguity over the principles and the specific language of the regulations, principles would prevail.

New provisions were prescribed in areas such as related-party transactions. Earlier, it was quite common for companies to buy or sell goods or services from companies that were owned and controlled by promoters or dominant shareholders. There was no mechanism to ensure that the terms of such transactions were not disadvantageous to the shareholders of the listed company. Often, assets of a listed company were sold to a promoter entity at throwaway prices with no checks and controls. The minority shareholders remained mute spectators. SEBI decided to implement a dramatic change in the power structure. The rules were altered to debar promoters and their associates from voting on transactions with related parties. The concept of majority of minority votes was introduced. In a way, majority shareholders were disempowered in matters where they would otherwise have been interested parties. While the government, media and a majority of corporate India supported these moves, some corporates protested angrily. An important industry leader famously commented that SEBI was behaving like a 'dragon' and most of them would be forced to leave the country to set up businesses abroad. But SEBI went ahead and implemented these measures. Nobody left India to set up shop abroad because of corporate governance requirements.

Enactment of the Companies Act, 2013, and the new corporate governance provisions by SEBI were very well appreciated and recognized by the whole world.[1] The ranking of India in shareholder protection in the World Bank report, which was number forty-nine in 2012, went up to number seven in 2016. Coupled with the growth of proxy advisory firms and adoption of a whistle-blower mechanism, this has brought India at the centre stage of the movement towards higher corporate governance. However, even today, instances of governance violations do often come to the fore, highlighting the need for continuous vigilance by regulators, shareholders and the media.

PART IV

Unregulated Deposit-taking Schemes

15

Collecting Deposits from the Public

One of the important issues before the country in the last two decades has been the growing incidence of unauthorized money, collection schemes. A huge amount of money has been collected for various misleading and dubious activities. While the effort to do so was pan-India, the areas most affected were West Bengal and the neigbhouring states in the eastern and north-eastern part of the country. The variety of the schemes was such that it was difficult for the public to make the fine distinction whether the money being deposited by them was actually for the delivery of goods or services such as housing, land and holidays, or it was an investment scheme in violation of laws and regulations. The fact that there are different authorities administering distinct activities, and these authorities have limited presence across the length and breadth of the country further complicated the situation.

Regulatory Vacuum

As there is no unified regulatory agency, operators work in a regulatory vacuum. A bank is allowed to raise deposits from the public. One major difference between banks and other institutions is that banks can issue 'on-demand deposits' whereas others can issue only 'time deposits'. Savings and current accounts can be opened by banks. Banks can issue cheque books. No other organization can do so.

Banks are licensed by the RBI and closely monitored by it. The RBI also supervises non-banking finance companies (NBFCs). Until 2008, NBFCs could raise deposits from the public. Companies registered under the Companies Act raise deposits from the public under certain conditions provided in the Act. Companies can also issue securities to the public and mobilize money. This activity is regulated by SEBI. Similarly, chit funds, which are operated under the Chit Funds Act of 1982, can accept deposits from their members. Another class is Nidhi funds. Cooperatives can similarly raise money from their members, but they are not permitted to raise money from the general public who are not members. Insurance schemes are regulated by Insurance Regulatory and Development Authority of India (IRDAI), pension schemes by PFRDA, and mutual funds, which can accept investments from the public, by SEBI. Cooperatives with operations across states are regulated under the Multi-State Cooperative Societies Act. The nodal ministry for this is the ministry of agriculture in the Government of India. Multilevel marketing companies operate under a law administered by the ministry of consumer affairs in the Government of India. In addition, in different times, there have been schemes for plantation, agricultural land, housing, timeshare in holiday homes, cattle- and bird-breeding, crop farming and a whole lot of other purposes. In view of the large variety of activities and multiplicity of regulatory authorities, it is difficult for even a well-educated person to decipher whether the scheme is genuine, legal and authorized and what are the protections available or where one can go in case of a complaint.

Past Policies

In the second half of the nineties, new developments took place across the country, where companies started mobilizing money from the general public for agricultural activities. They promised high returns ranging from 18 per cent to 30 per cent per year by issuing agri-bonds or plantation bonds. Schemes were marketed aggressively. Agents would market these bonds and offer very high commissions. Attractive media campaigns in print and newly available electronic media were launched. As agricultural income is not taxed, these plantation schemes promised investors that the income would be exempt from taxation. Tax-free returns became a major incentive for the public to invest in them.

The SEBI Act was amended in 1999 to provide for the regulation and supervision of collective investment schemes (CIS). Later, SEBI published detailed regulations for these schemes. It is, however, shocking that only one such scheme has been registered with SEBI in the last twenty years. In order to facilitate legitimate financial activities, several exemptions were provided in the Act from the definition of a CIS. These included chit funds, Nidhi funds, NBFCs, deposits raised under the Companies Act, mutual funds, pension funds and insurance companies.

These exemptions unwittingly provided much-needed loopholes for unscrupulous elements to launch their unauthorized schemes for mobilizing resources from the public without obtaining any permission or registration form from any authority like the RBI, SEBI, IRDA or MCA.

Chit Funds

The Chit Funds Act, 1982, is a Central Act implemented by the ministry of finance. These are classified as miscellaneous non-banking financial instruments under the RBI Act. The actual administration of the scheme is done by state governments, and officers are earmarked for registering and regulating the chit funds. Chit funds have been in existencc for decades and are very popular in the southern part of the country. These are meant to be only for members, and are close-ended schemes. The objective of these is to help grow the habit of thrift and savings.[1] There are about 25,000 chit funds doing a business of Rs 30,000 crore annually. However, several unregistered chit funds function in the country at the same time. The All India Association of Chit Funds (AIACF) estimated in 2005 that the total chit funds business would be Rs 50,000 crore annually.

Prize Chit Fund

A prize chit fund is a kind of chit fund that involves an element of speculation. It involves that all members were not entitled to get all their money back and at times less than 50 per cent receive their money. This is in contrast to a regular chit fund where all the members are assured of their money. Prize chit funds were banned by the Prize Chits and Money Circulation Schemes (Banning) (PCMCS) Act, 1978. Allied to these are money circulation schemes, where a promise is made to pay money on an event or contingency related to enrolment of members for the scheme. Many multilevel marketing schemes, which promise to pay money based on enrolment of members, also come under the purview of PCMCS Act.

Nidhi Company or Mutually Beneficial Company

Nidhis conduct the business of accepting deposits from and lending money to members only, not to outsiders. Nidhis cannot engage in the business of chit funds, hire purchase, insurance, etc., and are regulated under the Companies Act. These companies were created with the objective of cultivating the habit of thrift and savings amongst its members. RBI has exempted Nidhis from the core provisions of the RBI Act and other directions applicable to NBFCs. There are guidelines for their investments and also for the type of loans and securities against those loans that they can accept. A Nidhi company must have a net owned fund of Rs 10 lakh or more, and have at least 200 members.

Multi-state Cooperatives

Regulator-hopping

When the action around unregulated and unauthorized money collection schemes gathered momentum over 2011–14, a new avenue was chosen by many operators so as to beat the system and continue with fund mobilization. There had been an abnormal increase in the registration of multi-state cooperative credit and multipurpose societies during this period. These societies were functioning as autonomous organizations where the board of the society was empowered to undertake a business activity, which could include accepting deposits and giving loans to its members. But malpractices were taking place as there was no limit on the maximum number of members. Even nominal members could be included so deposits could be collected from them. As soon as pressure from SEBI mounted on certain organizations, many got registered as cooperative societies. Since they had collection across multiple states, conversion into multi-state cooperatives was the easiest route for them. Almost all big organizations, such as SRIL, MPS

Greenery Developers Ltd, PGF Ltd (PGFL), PACL, and even Sahara followed this practice.

A cooperative society is supposed to be servicing its members and not the public at large. Knowing the misuse of the provisions, some additional measures were taken to strengthen the registration process. It has now been decided that they can have operations initially only in two contiguous states or Union Territories and cannot accept deposits from nominal members. Earlier, the practice was to accept deposits from all and sundry, and include them as nominal members. This has now been disallowed.

Direct Selling Schemes

Direct selling is an alternative route of distribution and marketing of consumer products and services. Usually, it is done through the demonstration of the products by a direct seller. There is prevalence of this practice in many countries, including India. However, many multilevel marketing companies or direct selling companies were covered under the PCMCS Act. Because of the lack of clarity in the definition, some operators tried to run their incentives in a manner such that these appeared as financial pyramid schemes where incentives are given for recruiting more agents and not on the amount of the business actually received. The way this operates is that an agent is given a commission for recruiting more agents and appointing a new chain of agents. Often, the agents have to deposit certain amount of money and there is a promise of return at a certain rate of interest on these deposits. However, the agents don't have much protection in case the company refuses to pay or it winds up activity. Strangely, this subject comes under the ministry of consumer affairs in the Government of India and adds to one more layer of difficulty in coordination and integrated thinking about how to control unauthorized money collection.

The procedure of public issuance of securities is often violated by companies. They take a stand that what they are doing is a private placement and not a public issue. Sahara is the biggest example of this and will be delved into in more detail later in the book.

But this is not a complete list and ingenuity goes much beyond. Several novel methods have been adopted and new schemes launched in the last decade. Some of these schemes have played on the aspirations of the middle class in acquiring houses or owning holiday homes. Some have promised quick money in buying art or in rearing cattle and birds. Most of them were agile in changing their structures and moving funds from one type to another.

Common Thread

Most of these schemes have elements of a CIS. In order to avoid RBI supervision, these companies always claimed that they were not NBFCs. Obviously, these were not schemes of insurance, mutual funds or pension. They chose not to be registered as a CIS under the SEBI Act because their claim was that they were doing genuine business and not operating a financial scheme. All these schemes promised very high returns. In some cases, the promise was that the money would be doubled in two and a half to three years. The commission for agents was always high—as much as 20 per cent or 25 per cent. Nobody questioned what kind of legitimate business activity could guarantee that an investment of Rs 75 could become Rs 200 in three years! Lack of regulatory oversight, and low investor awareness combined to cause many people to invest in such schemes. In some cases, these companies also had popular brand ambassadors, glittering events and people in responsible positions—MPs and ministers—associated with them.

Unfortunately, at the operational level, there had been a trend of reluctance among the regulators to examine complaints expeditiously. There was a tendency to pass around the complaint to other regulators rather than applying their minds jointly and taking decisive action. A stand often taken in the regulatory institutions was that since the entity was not registered with them, they had no role to play in stopping these activities. At the same time, the mechanism for information-sharing and coordination was poor. In cases where SEBI started investigating and started asking questions from these companies, it was met with resistance and defiance. Courts also took time to appreciate the seriousness of the situation, and often the operators were able to take advantage of that situation.

16

Some Big Fish

During the course of my career, I witnessed multiple cases that involved loss of money for many people who had invested in the schemes of certain companies or entities. What is common to all of these is that the amount of money in question was very large, and these entities were operating across many states.

PGFL

A company was originally incorporated in the early 1980s as Pearl General Finance Ltd. It changed its name to Pearl Green Forest Ltd and finally to PGF Ltd. It was primarily running schemes involving the sale and purchase of agricultural land. In 1998, SEBI issued a show-cause notice to the company. The company's response was that its business was limited to the sale and purchase of agricultural land. It requested SEBI to drop all proceedings against the company. In February 2002, SEBI passed an order asking the company not to collect any more money from its customers or investors and to refund the money collected so far within a period of one month. PGFL moved the High Court of Punjab and Haryana, which stayed any further action against PGFL by an interim direction and finally directed SEBI to hear the matter afresh and determine the issue. After hearing them, a final order was passed in December 2002 directing PGFL to wind up its schemes and repay the investors within a period of one month and also to stop collecting any further money for its schemes. PGFL moved the high court again, challenging constitutional validity of the section in the SEBI Act dealing with CIS. This writ was dismissed by the high court in 2004. The company then appealed to the Supreme Court by filing a special leave petition (SLP) there. A final order was passed dismissing the SLP in March 2013.

Meanwhile, the company continued to collect money from investors with impunity and had a total amount close to Rs 15,000 crore. Until 2019, hardly any money has been recovered or refunded to its investors. SEBI had to move an application before the Supreme Court which was disposed off in 2015. The Supreme Court appointed a committee of two retired judges and asked that they supervise the sale of assets and disbursement to investors. The committee has been able to sell some of the movable properties of the company but selling the immovable properties and compensating the investors is still taking time.

PACL

Among the known cases of CIS, PACL is the one with the highest amount collected. It is also a case where a legal battle continued for the longest period of time—two decades. A PIL was filed in the Delhi High Court against various companies, including PACL, which were carrying on CIS activity without obtaining a certificate of registration from SEBI. Notices were served to PACL by SEBI. PACL approached the High Court of Delhi, which allowed the company to go ahead and execute sale deeds. Later, PACL filed a writ petition before the Rajasthan High Court. The high court first stayed the operation of SEBI's notice. Thereafter, in its final order of 2003, the high court held that none of the conditions under SEBI's CIS regulations were satisfied and quashed the notices. SEBI filed an appeal before the Supreme Court, which was finally decided in 2013. The Rajasthan High Court order was set aside. SEBI was asked to give the company a fresh hearing. Finally, in 2014, SEBI could pass an order holding the schemes of PACL as CIS. It asked the directors to wind up the schemes and refund the money. By then, the company had collected more than Rs 49,000 crore. The company went to SAT, where SEBI's orders were upheld. Against this order, they moved the Supreme Court.

In 2016, the Supreme Court set up a committee under the chairmanship of retired chief justice R.N. Lodha for disposing of the land purchased by the company so that the sale proceeds could be paid to the investors. Central Bureau of Investigation (CBI) was asked to hand over any documents that they had to SEBI.

It was, however, found that a majority of properties mentioned in the list were either in the possession of third parties, already sold or subject to dispute. In 80 per cent cases, the property documents were in the names of entities other than the company. In some cases, new construction had come up and third-party interest had been created. For example, in Rohini, New Delhi, where the company had got land allotted by Delhi Development Authority (DDA), it was found that a shopping mall had been constructed and transferred long before the constitution of the Lodha Committee. In Noida, as per the company's statement, 198 luxury flats had been sold off. However, documents did not reveal such status. In case of land at Samalkha, Panipat, it was informed that a total area of approximately twenty acres had already been sold. There were similar instances of contentious properties in Rajokri, New Delhi and Oshiwara, Mumbai.

Investigation revealed duplication of documents. In some cases, the state government of Maharashtra had acquired properties, while in others they had been attached by the income tax department. The income tax authority had passed an order imposing liability amounting to approximately Rs 24,500 crore. Other agencies such as Enforcement Directorate (ED) and the government of Andhra Pradesh had also attached properties. A lot of properties owned by the company had been given on lease. In order to safeguard illegal sale, letters were sent to inspectors general of registration in various states and to approximately 200 district magistrates to seek their help in not letting these properties be sold or names mutated in revenue records. The committee was also able to recover Rs 4080 crore worth of fixed-deposit receipts of various banks. It transpired that the company had acquired assets in Australia, causing the matter to be taken up in the Federal Court of Australia.

Alchemist Infra Realty Ltd

In 2011, SEBI received an anonymous letter about Alchemist Infra Realty Ltd. After ascertaining facts, a show-cause notice was issued to the company in 2012 and an order was passed in 2013 holding that the arrangements and operations of the company were CIS under the SEBI Act. They were asked to wind up the scheme and refund the money. The company applied for consent—a mechanism whereby, without admission of guilt, the individuals or companies can agree for a settlement amount to be given to SEBI and the case is closed. This mechanism is primarily meant for smaller offences and violations so that the efforts of SEBI can be directed towards other serious matters. As the corpus of default was large, the request for consent was rejected. This was challenged by them before SAT, which upheld SEBI's order. The company then asked eighteen months to wind up its schemes. It moved the Supreme Court but its appeal was dismissed as withdrawn. The company later informed authorities that out of the total of Rs 1900 crore, approximately Rs 177 crore has been refunded by them. They requested another twenty-four months to repay the balance. This was not accepted by SEBI, and it was moved to file prosecution against the company and its directors. Thereafter, recovery proceedings were initiated.

Rose Valley Group

Information was received from the Government of West Bengal that a company of the Rose Valley Group, namely Rose Valley Real Estates and Constructions Ltd (RVRECL), was collecting money from the public in West Bengal and neighbouring states through the Ashirbad scheme floated by it. Another company of the group, Rose Valley Resorts and Plantations Ltd (RVRPL), was running unauthorized CIS schemes since the late nineties. SEBI had rejected its application for registration as a valid CIS.[1]

The scheme involved selling a plot of land on a future date against money received in advance in instalments. If somebody did not want the land, a pre-determined credit value for the instalment paid was to be returned. The return promised to the investor was as high as 21 per cent. More than Rs 1200 crore had been collected under this scheme. It was discovered that actual plots of land were very few and in a vast majority of cases, it was really a scheme for earning high interest. In 2011, SEBI passed an order against the company and its directors asking them to desist from collecting money, and not to dispose of any property or divert funds.

In 2012, the information gathered regarding Rose Valley Hotels and Entertainment Ltd (RVHEL) and RVRECL stated that it had collected more than Rs 1000 crore in Assam and nearby states. The scheme was called Rose Valley Holiday Membership Plan (HMP). People could book a holiday package through payment in monthly instalments and upon maturity either avail of the facility or opt for a refund of investment along with interest. SEBI passed an interim order against the company. The company went to the Calcutta High Court, where its case was dismissed. But the company went to the division bench of the high court challenging the constitutional validity of SEBI Act and its CIS regulations. Through this they were given relief as the high court restrained SEBI from proceeding further. The company took advantage and continued raising money. SEBI then had to move the Supreme Court to direct the high court for an early hearing. When the Supreme Court did so, the matter was finally disposed of by the high court, upholding the constitutional validity of SEBI Act and the regulations, and dismissing the writ petition. SEBI could then pass orders against the company and its directors.

This case was also known for another reason. In 2010, CBI received a complaint that a deputy general manager of SEBI in Kolkata had demanded a bribe for preparing a report favourable to the company. CBI laid a trap, and the officer was caught red-handed accepting Rs 10 lakh. CBI started a criminal case against him and he was summarily dismissed from SEBI's employment.

Golden Forest (India) Ltd (GFIL)

This company was incorporated in 1987. By 1997, it had mobilized more than Rs 1000 crore and acquired more than 7000 acres of land. In 1998, an order was passed by SEBI asking it not to mobilize any further funds and prohibited it from selling or alienating any property. The order was not complied with. As a result, a writ was filed in the Bombay

High Court for directing banks to restrain the company from withdrawing any money. The high court asked for a committee of the RBI to be formed. The scheme formulated by the committee was approved by the court. A retired judge was appointed by the court to sell certain properties and repay the investors. Meanwhile, another case was going on in the High Court of Punjab and Haryana and several other courts. In view of the multiplicity of petitions in different high courts, SEBI approached the Supreme Court. In 2003, all the petitions were transferred to the Supreme Court. In 2004, an order was passed appointing another retired judge, along with an officer each nominated by the RBI and SEBI. Subsequently, other judges were appointed. Later, in 2010, these cases were transferred to the Delhi High Court. As on May 2016, an amount of Rs 700 crores was collected from the auction of properties of this group. Subsequently, the matter was again transferred to the Supreme Court in 2018. A new committee has been appointed and the case is still going on.

SRIL

Of all the unauthorized money collection schemes, this group acquired the maximum notoriety because of the important people directly and indirectly involved with it, and the sheer manner in which the events unfolded in this case. The company ran several schemes with maturity from twelve months to 180 months and different rates of interest. In case a person wanted refund of money instead of allotment of land or a flat, the company assured a refund with interest. The government of West Bengal sent information about the funds mobilization activities of Saradha Realty India Ltd (SRIL) to several Central authorities such as the RBI, MCA, SEBI, Economic Intelligence Council, etc. SEBI started examining whether CIS regulations could apply to it, and a show-cause notice was sent. One test that SEBI applied in many of these schemes was to see whether a larger proportion of members/ applicants actually opted for properties or asked for refund along with interest. If the latter was the case, it was held by SEBI that it was a CIS and not a real-estate activity. Similar facts emerged in SRIL.

When asked to submit papers, the company delayed. Later, as a strategy, they submitted cartons full of unrelated and irrelevant papers. The matter reached the Calcutta High Court, which asked them to send their representatives for verification. But no one appeared. In April 2013, an order was finally passed, deeming the activities of SRIL as a CIS and directing them to wind up the scheme and refund the money that had already been collected. They were debarred from accessing the capital market. Prosecution under SEBI Act was also lodged.

However, a few days before the order was passed by SEBI, the promoter of the group Sudipta Sen had made a lengthy disclosure about how he had siphoned off money, how some very important politicians were closely associated with various companies of the group and how middlemen had taken money from him for 'managing' different government authorities, including regulators such as the RBI, SEBI and MCA. Criminal cases were filed in other states as well, including Odisha. The government of West Bengal set up a judicial commission of inquiry into the different activities of this group. Meanwhile, a forensic audit of the group was conducted.

The names of important political personalities of different parties cropped up in these investigations. One MP wrote to the prime minister complaining about the activities of the group. After a few months, bizarrely, the same MP wrote another letter to the PM, claiming that his complaint had been made under some misguided impression. He said that he had made inquiries and was satisfied that the group was doing a good job.

Writ petitions were filed in the Supreme Court. In 2014, the court directed the cases from West Bengal and Odisha to be transferred to the CBI. The CBI has filed a series of charge sheets, and further investigation is still going on.

MPS Greenery Developers Ltd

In March 2000, MPS Greenery Developers Ltd applied for the grant of the certificate of registration under the SEBI (CIS) Regulations, 1999. It was rejected by SEBI. Thereafter, the company filed a writ petition before the Calcutta High Court, challenging SEBI's order. The high court, vide its interim order passed in 2002, directed that pending hearing, status quo be maintained regarding the affairs and functioning of the company. In 2006, information was received that the company continued to mobilize money. A contempt petition was filed in January 2007 against the company for continuing to raise funds from the schemes in violation of the status quo order of the high court passed in 2002. In 2009, the high court vacated the stay order.

A provisional registration certificate was granted by SEBI in 2009, under SEBI (CIS) Regulations. But the company was instructed to fulfil various conditions for a valid CIS and not to launch any new scheme or raise any money from the investors even under the existing scheme, unless a certificate of final registration had been granted to it. Since the company failed to fulfil the conditions laid down for provisional registration by SEBI, the provisional registration expired in August 2011.

Soon it was gathered that the company had collected money from the public even though it was prohibited from raising any money in any new or existing schemes. Accordingly, SEBI passed an interim order in May 2012 restraining MPS Greenery Developers Ltd from raising deposits from the public. Agents of the company filed collusive suits in district courts across the state of West Bengal. Even though district courts have no jurisdiction under the SEBI Act, in eight cases there were injunction orders restraining SEBI from further action. In clear violation of SEBI Act, such orders continued to pour in from district courts. SEBI had to approach these courts for vacating the injunction, and the company's stalling technique seemed to work perfectly. In many cases, SEBI officials faced harassment as the agents were local and strong in these district towns. The injunction orders were given ostensibly on the ground that the agents would lose their livelihood if the collection of deposits was stopped as per SEBI order. Nowhere else in the country has SEBI faced such repeated obstruction to its work from multiple district courts having no jurisdiction under law.

When SEBI issued a public advertisement cautioning investors, the company issued counter-advertisements claiming falsely that it had received the sanction of the court to raise money from the public. All of this was causing SEBI's authority to be undermined. Finally, SEBI was able to get the stay orders vacated in all the cases with great difficulty. In some scenarios, SEBI had to bring the matter before the high court and the Supreme Court. Subsequently, SEBI passed the final order in the matter in December 2012.

As a result of non-compliance of the SEBI order, prosecution was filed against the company and its directors in October 2013. Attachment and recovery proceedings were also initiated. Apprehending that the promoters/directors would flee the country after collecting a huge amount from the public, SEBI had to apply to the regional passport authority for impounding their passports. The request remained pending in the passport office. SEBI had to seek intervention of the Calcutta High Court in this matter. Finally, the regional passport authority intimated in 2015 that the passports of the directors of MPS Greenery Developers Ltd would be impounded. The Calcutta High Court appointed a retired judge in December 2015 as a one-man committee to, inter alia, auction the movable and immovable properties of MPS Group and to refund the investors.

This case provides a glimpse of the difficulties faced at different levels right from the district court and the passport office to the higher judiciary. Not only that, the impunity of those raising money for years together was evident in the manner they challenged the action of SEBI through advertisements in the media.

Strengthening Laws and Ensuring Coordination

One important common inference from all these cases is that once the operators have been allowed to mobilize money from public, it has taken an unusually long time for the regulatory and judicial system to recover the money and restore the same to the investors. Almost all the cases landed up in high courts and the Supreme Court. A delay of up to a decade or even beyond was not uncommon. Matters had to be taken up right from the district courts to the Supreme Court, from state governments to the passport office. Even after the success in courts, actual recovery of money was negligible, and refunds to investors have been far from satisfactory.

The learning is that since multiple laws and different agencies are involved, the need is to have effective and continuous coordination. The coordination mechanism at the highest level is the FSDC. It is headed by the finance minister and includes the governor of the RBI, finance secretary and head of other regulatory bodies such as SEBI, IRDAI, PFRDA, etc. For coordination at the operational level, there is a sub-committee of the FSDC (FSDC-SC) chaired by the RBI governor. As early as June 2012, I presented a paper to the FSDC-SC highlighting how operators were able to raise money from gullible investors by taking advantage of the loopholes in legal provisions and the lack of clarity about the role of different agencies. The paper argued for bringing the whole matter under a principal regulator for all cases where pooling of money from numerous investors was taking place. It was pointed out that there was a need to provide criteria, such as the maximum numbers of investors or the maximum amount collected, beyond which all operators would have to compulsorily get registered with the principal regulator. Also, in cases where there was no defined regulatory authority, the principal regulator would be deemed to have the authority. A new legislation to deal with the menace was proposed. In the interim, the paper suggested the creation of a mechanism for information-sharing and coordination in which the RBI, SEBI, MCA and state governments should be members. This issue was further raised by SEBI in the FSDC meeting held in November 2012, followed by a letter to the finance minister in the same month. The need for a principal regulator, a coordination mechanism at the state level, and strengthening the enforcement powers of SEBI were issues that were taken up.

Amendment of SEBI Act

Finally, SEBI's points were accepted by the Central government in 2013. Realizing the gravity of the matter, finance minister Chidambaram ensured that an ordinance was issued incorporating these charges in the SEBI Act. This is one of the rare examples where the ordinance was promulgated thrice as the government could not get the same passed in the Parliament before the 2014 Lok Sabha elections. The bone of contention was the proposal for giving powers of search and seizure to SEBI without going to a court of law. The new finance minister, Jaitley, came out with a solution to the issue and the amendment was finally cleared by the Parliament in August 2014.

It was clarified that any pooling of funds under any scheme or arrangements not registered with SEBI or other regulators in the financial sector, and with a corpus of Rs 100 crore or more, would be deemed to be a CIS. The earlier defence available to unscrupulous elements was taken away. Now the operators would have to prove that their scheme had due approval from authorities like SEBI, the RBI, IRDA, MCA or the state government.

There were several instances where the companies collecting money did not cooperate and avoided or delayed the submission of documents, records and accounts. This amendment also empowered SEBI to call for any relevant information from any authority or any individual. The power given allowed SEBI to call for information from authorities even outside India. One shortcoming frequently noticed in the past was that while SEBI could issue an order and direct the companies to stop collecting money or even impose monetary penalty, there was no way money could be restored to investors if the assets of the company were not sufficient. But the 2014 amendment also gave SEBI powers of disgorgement. Now there were legal powers to recover money from other assets of the defaulters and restore it to the individuals.

Earlier, when SEBI imposed penalties, it had to file a recovery proceeding in a civil court, and actual recovery took fifteen to twenty years. The culprits knew that recovery orders were not likely to be practically enforced. However, this amendment gave the power of recovery to a SEBI officer, to attach and sell movable and immovable property of the concerned person, attach his bank account and even arrest the person and detain him in prison. This powerful provision has served as a deterrent. The SEBI Act even has a provision that, in serious cases, SEBI could file criminal complaints against the offenders. Earlier, as there was no designated court, actual punishment was a long drawn-out matter. This amendment created a designated court and all cases could be filed here. This is again a very helpful amendment that could bring a culprit to justice far sooner than before.

State Protection of Interest of Depositors Act

In 1997, the government of Tamil Nadu enacted a legislation to protect the interests of depositors. This was a novel move. As banking, deposit-taking and related subjects were a part of the lawmaking powers of the Central government, there was some uncertainty around its validity. The Act was challenged before the Supreme Court, which held that the object was to ameliorate the situation of thousands of depositors from the clutches of financial establishments who had duped the public. The court held that the Act was not focused on transactions of banking or acceptance of deposits, but designed to protect the public from fraudulent financial establishments. Therefore, the Act was held to be constitutionally valid. Other states like Maharashtra followed suit. But many states, most notably West Bengal, did not have the legislation until as late as 2014.

These Acts define a financial establishment as any entity accepting deposits under any scheme or arrangement and in any manner. Financial establishments are prohibited from accepting any deposits either in cash or in kind. Any fraudulent default in repayment of deposits invites imprisonment of up to six years and a monetary penalty. The government can attach the money or any property of these establishments. District authorities have been given substantial powers to stop unauthorized collection. Designated courts can pass an order for attachment of properties and equitable distribution among the depositors. Money can also be recovered from those to whom the money or the proceeds of CIS have been transferred.

The RBI and SEBI encouraged states to pass such laws, and several of them did so. However, it took quite some time for the government of West Bengal to pass such a law. Even after the bill was passed by the West Bengal legislature, it took an unusually long time for the government of India to process it for the assent of the president. Finally, the law is in place.

As of 2019, twenty-seven states and Union Territories have enacted laws to protect the interest of depositors. Among the large states, only Rajasthan had not yet enacted the legislation, till the middle of 2019.

Report of the Parliamentary Standing Committee on Finance

The working of various departments and ministries of the government of India and the institutions within those ministries/departments are reviewed by different standing committees of the Parliament. In the Sixteenth Lok Sabha, the standing committee on the ministries of finance and corporate affairs examined the regulation of CIS and other money collection schemes in great detail. In the twenty-first report of this committee headed by Veerappa Moily, submitted in September 2015, several important recommendations were imposed.[2] These include:

- The government should launch a country-wide financial literacy and awareness campaign.
- Since advantage of regulatory vacuum/lacunae is being taken by entities to raise large amount, of money from

gullible people, appropriate legislative provisions should be brought in without delay.

- The state government machinery should be utilized to gather market intelligence. Coordinated action by concerned regulators and agencies at different centralized levels is required.
- A Central legislation may be enacted incorporating the best features of the state Acts. The state Acts, then, may be accordingly amended in line with the Central law.
- The jurisdiction of special courts under SEBI Act should be expanded to cover offences of unauthorized money collection as well.

Banning Unregulated Deposit Schemes Ordinance, 2019

Realizing the seriousness of unregulated deposit schemes, based on the recommendations of the standing committee of the Parliament, the government promulgated an ordinance on 21 February 2019. The bill for this legislation was passed by the Lok Sabha but it could not be taken up in the Rajya Sabha immediately. So the government decided to promulgate an ordinance. The scheme of this Act states that all unregulated deposit schemes shall be banned. The state government as well as the Central government has jurisdiction over the matter. In case anybody solicits money in contravention of the Act, an officer of the government can attach the deposits held by the agency or any other property acquired by them, and designated courts can be established for the trial of offences. There is also a provision for restitution of the money to depositors. For offences such as soliciting deposits, accepting deposits or defaulting on repayment of such deposits, even imprisonment is provided. The ordinance extends even to the publication of advertisements of unregulated deposit schemes and may require the concerned newspaper to retract the information free of cost. After the 2019 elections, the bill has been passed by both houses of the Parliament.

Primarily, this law has the best feature of some of the state laws. The combination of the amended SEBI Act, which has a deeming provision of a scheme being considered a CIS if the money collected is Rs 100 crore or more, and the new Depositors' Protection Act has plugged the loopholes in dealing with the menace. However, as the gold deposit scheme of Karnataka in 2019 has demonstrated, all the public authorities have to work in a coordinated manner to stop the repeat of such activities.

17

Deemed Public Issue—Sahara

Some companies in the past have chosen to take the route of making unauthorized and irregular collections of funds from the public through public issue of shares and debentures without following the process prescribed for it by law. The general philosophy followed in drafting legislation has been that if a company is raising money either from its existing shareholders or from a limited number of new subscribers, who may be friends, relatives, associates or employees, by issuing securities (shares or debentures) to them, then the procedural requirement need not be onerous. Since the number of subscribers is limited in such a private placement and they know the company well, the concern about the safety of their investment is limited. However, when the resources are raised by issuing securities to a large number of people, a more stringent diligence and disclosure have to be followed.

In such a case, a draft prospectus has to be issued to state to the public the important information about the financial health of the company, its nature of business and the objective of fundraising. It ought to have certification from directors and auditors. Apart from this, a number of other information points relevant for the members of the public to take an informed decision have to be disclosed. The general public is given an opportunity to offer comments or raise questions on the draft prospectus. SEBI can offer its comments too. A public issue has to have an opening and a closing date, beyond which further money cannot be collected. The securities so issued have to be listed on a stock exchange. There is a criminal liability for untrue statements made to the public or for misleading inclusions or omissions. In addition, there are civil liabilities on the promoters and directors of such companies. If funds are collected from fifty or more individuals, the law presumes that it is a deemed public issue, and all the requirements of a public issue have to be followed or serious consequences can befall those responsible for the fundraising

In spite of clear legal provisions, many companies have deliberately resorted to raising funds from hundreds of thousands of members of the public by taking recourse to the private placement route, even though it was restricted for issue made to less than fifty subscribers. The maximum number of subscribers in a private placement has now been enhanced to 200 under the Companies Act, 2013. The main intention of companies that violate this rule has been to mislead investors and avoid stricter public scrutiny. Subscribers are denied full information about the true financial condition of the company and its actual business. They are not aware of how much money is being raised, how many subscribers there are, the duration of the issue, or the corporate purpose for it. In addition, there is often a strong push from agents and salesmen. Investors are often duped into making these investments without any idea about the risk factors, or the remedy or guarantee available to them in case of refund or redemption.

In most cases, the preferred instrument is debt instead of equity. Generally, debentures or bonds (both terms are used interchangeably) are issued as these contain provisions of an assured rate of interest. People find these assurances very attractive. The rates of interest offered are very high so that these debentures can be easily sold. Several complications can be built into these instruments. A debenture can be convertible into equity, either partially or fully. The conversion into equity shares can take place at the option of the investor, compulsorily after a period or be linked to an event in future, such as the share prices of the company crossing a certain band. But, instead of highlighting these complications, agents push the instrument on the strength of the high rate of interest being offered.

Although many companies have taken recourse to it, the Sahara case is the biggest example in the country of a deemed public issuance. The surprising fact, however, is that neither SEBI nor any other government agency, such as the RBI or MCA, raised any red flag about such a large amount of money being raised from the public in utter violation of the law. Had Sahara Prime City Ltd (a group company) not decided to list on the stock exchange and thereby be forced to make disclosures to SEBI regarding its group entities such as Sahara India Real Estate Corporation Ltd (SIRECL) and Sahara Housing Investment Corporation Ltd (SHICL), the matter would never have come to light. It is also significant that the process of issuing these optionally fully convertible debentures (OFCDs) started around the same time as the RBI placed severe restrictions on the working of Sahara India Financial Corporation Ltd (SIFCL), a non-banking finance company of the group. SIFCL had been asked by the RBI not to raise any fresh deposits from the public and to close all existing deposits and reduce its public liability to nil in a given time frame.[1] It is no coincidence that around the same time, these new instruments were issued by two companies of the Sahara group.

According to their own admission, the net amount raised by the two companies was more than Rs 24,000 crore from more than three crore investors.

Interim Order by SEBI

The SEBI Act states that in the interest of preventing continuing harm to investors, the regulator can pass an interim order pending conclusion of investigation. The bonds issued by SHICL were so open-ended that, although the issuance began in 2008, even in 2010 subscription was still possible. In view of this, SEBI passed an interim order in November 2010 restricting SIRECL and SHICL from mobilizing further funds under the red-herring prospectus issued by them in March 2008 and October 2009 respectively. They were further restrained from offering any shares or debentures to the public or even inviting subscription until further directions.

This sparked off one of the most keenly watched and widely reported legal battles in the history of this country. Although nine years have elapsed since the first order (interim) was passed, the case is still not over. It has tested not only the powers and authority of SEBI, but also how the directions of the highest court of this land, the Supreme Court, can be frustrated with impunity.

In December 2010, Sahara approached the Lucknow bench of Allahabad High Court in a writ petition and received a stay against the interim order of SEBI. Many in SEBI felt that this was a setback. The regulator had no option but to approach the Supreme Court. In its order passed in January 2011, the Supreme Court directed the high court to proceed with the hearing on a day-to-day basis. It also clarified that SEBI would be entitled to continue with its inquiry. In April 2011, the Lucknow bench of the Allahabad High Court finally passed an order vacating the stay it had granted earlier. The observations in this order are important to note. The court was dismayed at the fact that the assurances given before the court by Sahara were not honoured by them. It said: 'The court's orders cannot be allowed to be violated or circumvented by any means.' Sahara filed another petition in the high court to restore the stay order. This was also rejected with the observation that 'if assurance is given by any person to the court, as has been done in the present case, and the said assurance/understanding is not honoured, the court would not come to his rescue.'

Final Order by SEBI (June 2011)

There was a sense of jubilation in SEBI at the new high court order. It was an endorsement of what SEBI was doing. Sahara went to the Supreme Court against this order. The Supreme Court in May 2011 asked SEBI, as the custodian of investors' interest and an expert body, to examine the issues expeditiously and pass appropriate orders. However, the same would not be given effect until the Supreme Court decided the matter.

In light of the above, Whole-time Member of SEBI K.M. Abraham passed the final order in June 2011. This was less than a month before his stint at SEBI came to an end. It was a comprehensive order in which each and every point of the law and fact was effectively dealt with. It clearly established which provisions of different laws/regulations had been violated, and how SEBI had the jurisdiction to deal with the case even though the concerned companies were not listed on the stock exchange. This order became the foundation for appeal before SAT and then before the Supreme Court by Sahara.

The case before the Supreme Court is still not resolved. Some of the important points made in SEBI's order of 23 June 2011 are that in June 2008, the RBI had issued a direction to SIFCL, a residual non-banking company (RNBC), prohibiting it from accepting any fresh deposit maturing beyond 30 June 2011. Since the minimum tenure of the deposits could be twelve months, effectively, it restrained

SIFCL from raising fresh deposits beyond 30 June 2010. SIFCL was also to stop accepting instalments on existing deposits. They were asked to bring down their liabilities towards the general public to zero by 30 June 2015. It was noted that the scheme by SIFCL was similar to a recurring deposit scheme, and the mobilization had taken place through thousands of agents all over the country. At the same time, the OFCD scheme had no firm closing dates and was almost similar to running an account in the nature of a passbook akin to a para-banking activity.

SEBI held that the OFCDs raised by these two companies were no different from deposits from the public, except that there was an option to convert these into equity shares. The details of the investors had not been publicly disclosed, and it was also noted that there were reports that the Sahara companies were now planning to use a third method of fund mobilization, i.e. through cooperative societies. SEBI held that the OFCDs issued by the two companies fell within their jurisdiction. These had been issued to more than fifty individuals and were of public issuance in nature. These funds had been raised in violation of the law. These two companies were not eligible to make a public offer, as no draft offer document was filed, no debenture trust deed for securing these debentures was executed, no debenture redemption reserve was created, no monitoring agency was appointed to oversee, and no credit rating was conducted. The issues were kept open for more than two years in contravention of the time limit of ten days. They had failed to apply and obtain permission to list on the stock exchange. SEBI, therefore, ordered the two companies and their directors to refund the money collected, along with 15 per cent annual interest from the date of receipt of the money until such repayment. They were restrained from accessing the securities market for raising further funds until the refunds had taken place. They were also restrained from associating themselves with any listed company.

The Supreme Court Order (August 2012)

Abraham left SEBI in July 2011, when his deputation from the government of Kerala came to an end. This subject matter came to be handled by Prashant Sharan, a veteran from the RBI who had joined SEBI two years earlier. He was ably assisted on the operations side by S. Ravindran and on the legal side by J. Ranganayakulu—both executive directors. Sahara appealed before SAT. The appeal was dismissed. It then went to the Supreme Court. The final order of the Supreme Court was delivered on 31 August 2012.

There are three or four very important aspects of the Supreme Court order, which need to be observed carefully. Generally, in similar matters, a regulatory authority like the RBI or SEBI issues a direction to the concerned entity to refund the money directly to the subscribers, with or without payment of interest. When the RBI took a decision regarding Peerless or Sahara, it asked the concerned companies to refund the money. Even the order passed by SEBI in the case of the Sahara companies in June 2011 asked them to make the payments directly to the investors. No such order had ever been passed that the funds collected have to be deposited with a regulator like SEBI. In the earlier situation, the company raising funds has the leeway to provide a certificate of payment without the regulator examining the actual payment in great detail. Past history shows that unless there are serious complaints, the regulators believe the fundraising company, and their certification, ends the matter. In this situation, the company can either actually refund the money in full or in part or convert the deposit into some other instrument partially or fully.

By doing so they can technically comply with the requirement of repayment to the original investors. But the special feature of the order of the Supreme Court in this matter was asking the Sahara companies to deposit the entire money with SEBI as well as to furnish within ten days, all the documents of fund collection and repayment/redemption to SEBI for verification. From the date of the order, they were actually prevented from making any payment directly to the investors. It became SEBI's task, as per this order, to verify the actual investors and repay them. Thus, the Sahara companies lost the flexibility of taking a stand on a later date that they had paid back all the investors. One of the reasons for the Supreme Court to take such a stand may have been their conviction that there may not be actual investors. The Supreme Court had expressed its surprise that some addresses were incomplete and not as per the prevailing practice in the country, and put forth the idea that even some of the names might be fictitious. The real problem for Sahara began because of this direction. Even the RBI had earlier felt that KYC norms were not strictly followed by the Sahara companies and that their records were haphazard.

This aspect of the Supreme Court order was the real game-changer. All their records and accounts came under public scrutiny, as part of an order passed by the highest court of the country. A retired Supreme Court judge, Justice B.N. Agrawal, was appointed to monitor the implementation of the order. SEBI could seek guidance from him from time to time.

Implementation of the Supreme Court Order

The first task for the Sahara companies was to deposit all the relevant records and documents with SEBI within ten days, i.e. by 10 September 2012. However, each development in the case was accompanied by high drama, and the companies lodged a letter alleging that one of their officers who had gone to meet SEBI officials was wrongfully detained and not allowed to leave the SEBI office even after office hours. There was even obstruction in the delivery of letters from SEBI to Sahara. Within three days of the Supreme Court order, the Sahara companies wrote to SEBI that because of the media highlighting the Supreme Court order, there was a sudden flood of investors at their branches and they had no option but to pay them. They were promptly told to follow the specific directions of the court and send the papers to SEBI in a structured format. The details of SEBI officials dealing with the matter were also provided to them. Strangely, they refused to take the hand delivery of SEBI's letter of 6 September. A fax was tried but their fax machine was found to be not in order. Ultimately the communication had to be sent by speed-post. Two of their representatives, Saurabh Bhattacharya and Kuldeep Singh, visited SEBI office on 10 September. This was the last date given to them by the Supreme Court for supplying all the relevant documents to SEBI. One of the reasons for their visit was to find out whether SEBI was willing to accept submission of documents beyond 10 September. They were told that SEBI had no authority to bypass the Supreme Court order. Bhattacharya left the SEBI office and Singh refused to receive SEBI's letter. Seventeen attempts were made to contact Bhattacharya on his mobile phone but every time the call was disconnected. Transmission by fax was tried but the same was not found to be in order and finally the letter had to be sent by speed-post on 11 September. Finally, only one truck containing documents arrived at around 8 p.m. on 10 September (the last day for receiving papers) outside the gate of SEBI office and after office hours. SEBI refused to accept this.

The next day, the Sahara companies complained that their officer was wrongfully confined by SEBI officials and not allowed to leave. But the discrepancies did not end there. SEBI received complaints that there were attempts to forcibly convert the OFCDs into other instruments of Sahara, such as an instrument of Sahara Credit Cooperative Society Ltd (SCCSL), and Sahara Q Shop Unique Products Range Ltd (SQSUPRL). The idea would have been to present to SEBI or the Supreme Court that the original holders of the OFCDs had been paid off. An advertisement had to be issued by SEBI in newspapers, asking the public not to be coerced by Sahara officials and forcibly convert their OFCDs. Since these conversions were reportedly taking place without consent, SEBI took up the matter with the chief secretaries of Uttar Pradesh and Maharashtra. SEBI issued directions to Sahara to provide information about the bank accounts where the OFCD money was deposited, the accounts where the money was transferred and also information about all their movable and immovable assets.

The directions of the Supreme Court regarding the deposit of papers connected with the investors were not followed in time. In spite of being prohibited from making any payments directly, Sahara informed that, due to a huge rush at their branches, they had been repaying directly. SEBI filed a contempt petition in the Supreme Court.

Receipt of Documents and Money from Saharas

There were two appeals before SAT against SEBI's refusal to extend the deadline for filing documents. The appeals were dismissed by SAT. The companies also communicated to SAT that they were ready with the money but their apprehension was that SEBI would refuse to accept it. The matter again reached the Supreme Court. A demand draft of Rs 5120 crore was produced before the Supreme Court. The Court extended the timeline for submitting the documents within the next fifteen days, until 5 December 2012, and also asked them to deposit Rs 5120 crore immediately and the balance in two instalments. The first instalment of Rs 10,000 crore was to be paid within the first week of January 2013 and the entire balance amount along with the up-to-date interest within the first week of February 2013.

The documents started arriving from 10 December and a total of 127 truckloads came. These trucks contained more than 31,000 cartons of paper. Inside SEBI, there was worry, and outside in the media there was intense speculation, about how SEBI would store these voluminous documents, segregate them and verify them. A team consisting of S. Ravindran, executive director, and Sunil Kumar, chief general manager (CGM), had already conducted a detailed survey. They finally zeroed down on a warehouse of SHCIL in Mapase, Navi Mumbai. This was a very modern building, with a large storage facility and a state-of-the-art document retrieval system.

Tamal Bandyopadhyay, in his book *Sahara: The Untold Story*, estimates that if the documents were laid out in a single line, it would have stretched to 6300 km.[2] The documents were delivered in a very haphazard manner. In many cases, different pages of the same documents were kept in different cartons. However, in spite of these difficulties, SEBI began the work of rearranging them and digitizing them. Later, V.S. Sundaresan, CGM, joined this team and carried on the task.

Inconsistencies

There were several inconsistencies in the stand taken by the Sahara companies from time to time. This was pointed out by SEBI through an affidavit filed in the contempt petition initiated by it. As early as January 2012, they had taken a stand that there were more than three crore investors whose funds had been safely invested in various immovable assets. It stated that there was no need for any repayment as redemption would be required only after 2018.

In June 2012, the group took the stand that the principal outstanding liability of SIRECL was Rs 16,997 crore, and that of SHICL, Rs 6352 crore.

In January 2014, it stated that it had carried on a divestment programme, and in just two months, May and June 2012, the two companies had refunded the investors close to Rs 16,000 crore. But if this was actually correct, it was neither reported to the Supreme Court in June 2012, nor to SAT in November 2012 or even in 2013.

On the contrary, the very next day after the Supreme Court order in August 2012, an advertisement issued by the companies in various newspapers mentioned that they would refund all the money as directed by the Supreme Court. There was no mention that close to Rs 16,000 crore had already been refunded by June 2012. Besides, their argument was that they had done so by divesting their assets and investment. If that was actually the case, there was no basis to contend that all their investments were intact. When asked to show the details of payments, they stated that all refunds had been made in cash, despite the directive stating that it was to make the refund through the banking channel.

Another contradiction in their claim was that they had received Rs 6366.66 crore from Sahara Q Shop, of which Rs 5120 crore had been paid to SEBI. The money had been paid in May, June and July 2012, when Sahara Q Shop actually began its business only in August 2012! According to them, between May 2012 and March 2013, SIRECL and SHICL had paid Rs 19,989.87 crore to SIRECL and Rs 5209.53 crore to SHICL, bringing the total to Rs. 25,199.40 crore. Out of this, close to

Rs 21,000 crore was mobilized in the first four months, between May 2012 and August 2012. That is, the mobilization from group companies for repayment to investors was almost complete even before the Supreme Court had passed its first order.

However, Sahara issued advertisements in newspapers on 16 February 2013 and 18 February 2013, claiming to have refunded Rs 22,117.39 crore, and that the outstanding liability was Rs 3363.93 crore. It also claimed that 50 per cent of this amount was no longer an outstanding liability since they had repaid investors in distant rural areas and were in the process of verification. It was also claimed that since they had already deposited Rs 5120 crore with SEBI, they were eligible for a big refund. On trying to determine whether payments had actually been made by cash, no entries were found in the cash book. Even in cases where refund was stated to have been made by cheques, the bank books did not contain any such references. A prima facie examination also brought out that there were at least fifty instances where the repayment vouchers were found to be pre-dated, i.e. prior to the request made by the bondholder for repayment.

Where Are the Investors?

The court doubted that there were actually as many investors as had been claimed. This aspect is further exacerbated by the fact that the court took the unusual step of asking SEBI to deposit the unspent money with the government of India in case there was no pending claim from investors. Going by the principal amount collected by Sahara and not counting the interest accrued, the fiscal position of the government would have improved by more than Rs 25,000 crore!

Subsequent developments further strengthened this belief. Before passing the order in June 2011, SEBI had done a pilot test in Mumbai of only four investors and found that two of them declined from having made any such investment. The other two mentioned that they were persuaded by the agents of Sahara. Only 50 per cent of the sample set accepted that they had investments and that too not because they were part of Sahara India Pariwar. It was not a private placement, and important people of their locality working as agents of Sahara had persuaded them.

Later, SEBI had received more than 2500 complaints from investors about their repayments. Some of these complaints were about being coerced by Sahara or its agents to convert their bonds into new instruments. In January 2013, SEBI issued redemption notices to a sample of 21,253 OFCD holders selected randomly; 7652 of these were returned undelivered because the addresses were either incomplete or wrong. In 3355 cases, no response was received. Out of the letters actually delivered, only in 246 cases was the response received, along with the relevant details. This number accounted for the mere 1.2 per cent people to whom communication was sent out. This further strengthened the suspicion about actual number of investors that Sahara group companies were claiming.

From May 2013, repeated advertisements were issued by SEBI, asking people to apply to it for redemption. In spite of 195 ads in multiple newspapers in different languages across the country across six months, only 3375 applications for refund amounting to Rs 25.37 crore were received. Even here more than 50 per cent (1816) were found to be disputed in nature as the claim did not match the records submitted by Sahara. It is difficult to believe that somebody having actually made investment in a scheme of a company would not respond to the request of a public authority to come forward and claim their money. This seems a more likely scenario if the names provided to SEBI are fictitious and non-existent.

Or alternatively, they must already have received their payments. Sahara made the plea that investors were not responding to SEBI's regular advertisements for raising claims because they had already received their money and had no grievances. But if that was the case, the Sahara companies should have been able to produce the required documents to prove it. In spite of several opportunities given to them, they could not provide the actual number of cases or the actual amount or the bank account and dates on which these payments had been made.

Enough Is Enough

Strict compliance by SEBI of the orders passed by the Supreme Court, with the action being monitored by a retired Supreme Court judge appointed by the court and regular filing of status reports by SEBI in the Supreme Court frustrated the Sahara group. Other courts in the country also cooperated. The high court of Himachal Pradesh, for example, passed an order in March 2013 restraining five entities—Sahara India Pariwar, Subrata Roy Sahara, SCCSL, SQSUPRL and Sahara Q Gold Mart Ltd (SQGML)—from raising money from the public for any of their schemes in the state of Himachal Pradesh. In another writ petition filed by Sahara before the Lucknow bench of Allahabad High Court challenging certain orders of SEBI, the high court in March 2013 advised SEBI to seek clarification from the Supreme Court.

This frustration resulted in the full-page advertisements being released by the group on 17 March 2013 with the headline 'Enough Is Enough'.[3] Invoking Bharat Maa, it was alleged that SEBI was continuously damaging its hard-earned and clean image by deliberately framing wrong orders. It stated that SEBI was working under the dictates of powerful third parties and such acts were mala fide. They held out a challenge and invited the chairman or other officers of SEBI for a live debate with Subrata Roy Sahara on a TV channel, to let people know what wrong had been committed by SEBI. There was also anguish in that ad that he had written personally to me—thrice—for an appointment, but his requests had not been entertained.

The group didn't stop at this advertisement. There were reports in newspapers that Subrata Roy Sahara, the chairman and managing worker, had complained that SEBI was working like a 'sarkari gunda'.[4] In spite of these provocations, SEBI decided to stay on course, not to take any of these allegations personally, and continued to work as per the law and the directions of the Supreme Court. The matter, however, did not end here and took some interesting twists and turns.

18

The Tightening Noose

Further Developments

Another contempt petition was filed by SEBI in February 2013 as Sahara had not implemented the directions of 5 December 2012 by the Supreme Court. SEBI also passed orders against SIRECL and SHICL and their directors/promoters to attach their movable and immovable properties, and bank accounts. The details of properties had not been furnished. Roy and other directors were asked to appear in person for examination and produce title deeds. When they finally appeared in the courtroom of Prashant Sharan on 10 April 2013, they did not produce the documents that had been asked for. In his affidavit, Roy asserted that he had no immovable property. After coming out of SEBI, he famously told the waiting media that not even a cup of tea had been offered to him.

SEBI wrote to eighty-eight commercial banks, 1434 urban cooperative banks, 380 systematically important NBFCs, mutual funds and depositories. The total amount transferred to SEBI was less than Rs 20 crore and that frozen by mutual funds approximately Rs 26 crore. The two depositories had frozen twelve demat accounts. Information was received from PNB that the net worth of Roy was Rs 4021.65 crore towards the end of March 2011. This information had been provided to them in the context of an application for a term loan for a residential project in Nagpur by Sahara Prime City Ltd. SEBI had started the practice of submitting status reports to the Supreme Court from time to time. Each report was vetted by Justice Agrawal.

In one the reports submitted in March 2013, a request was made on behalf of SEBI that as the non-recovery of dues would be a loss to the public exchequer, it would be just and expedient that the promoter of Sahara and its male directors be placed in civil prison. Meanwhile miscellaneous petitions were being filed in SAT and in different high courts. In July 2013, the Supreme Court ordered that no high court or any other forum could pass any directions against the orders passed by SEBI in compliance of the Supreme Court order.

During the hearing of the contempt petition before the Supreme Court, representatives of Sahara offered to provide SEBI the original title deeds of unencumbered properties worth Rs 20,000 crore as well as valuation reports within three weeks. This was accepted by the court but senior officers of the group were restrained from travelling abroad without the permission of the court. The court also asked the Sahara companies to produce records and bank details in support of their claim that they had made refunds of more than Rs 22,000 crore. Their plea was that all payments had been made in cash, and hence there were no bank details to furnish.

In view of the conflicting stands and the defiant attitude of Sahara, the court asked for the personal appearance of the contemnors before it on 26 February 2014. Exemption of the appearance of Roy Sahara was sought on the grounds that his mother was ill. This request was declined. Upon his non-appearance, a non-bailable warrant was issued against Roy. Finally, on 4 March 2014, the court observed that the contemnors had been taking an unreasonable stand in the case throughout. Their claim of having made refunds stood falsified by their own affidavits and documents furnished by them. Invoking the powers under Articles 129 and 142 of the Constitution, they ordered the detention of Roy Sahara, Ashok Roy Choudhary and Ravi Shankar Dubey. Vandana Bhargava, being a woman director, was exempt from detention. She was permitted to be in touch with those detained so that they could submit an acceptable proposal for the refund of money.

Request for Bail

The focus thereafter shifted to the contemnors obtaining bail. An order was passed to grant interim bail on the condition that they would pay Rs 10,000 crore, out of which Rs 5000 crore was to be deposited before the court and a bank guarantee of a nationalized bank for the balance could be produced. First, the order of detention was challenged by them as being void. This petition was dismissed. Then a plea was made to lift the earlier restrictions imposed on the operation of their bank and demat accounts. Similar restrictions imposed on movable and immovable properties were also sought to be removed on the condition that the net proceeds could be used for the compliance of the court orders.

The group was allowed by the court to encash its fixed deposits, bonds and securities and deposit the money with SEBI. It was also allowed to sell properties in nine different cities as per the list given by them, but at a price not lower than that indicated by them before the court. It was also clarified that the buyers should not be related to Sahara. They were also allowed to create a charge on their properties in Aamby Valley (near Pune) for the purpose of getting a bank guarantee. The Sahara companies had also provided information about their properties outside India, viz. Grosvenor House in London, and Plaza Hotel and Dream Downtown Hotel in New York. Together, the realizable value for Sahara from these three properties was estimated to be more than Rs 5000 crore. The Court asked for more information on these properties before they could take a call.

Facilities in Jail

The group continued with its plea that its effort to sell the properties and pay up was being hampered because its decision-makers were in jail. The Supreme Court acceded to a very unusual request to provide conference facilities inside the jail premises with all the modern communication equipment and secretarial assistance. On the plea that prospective buyers or their advisors were living in different parts of the world in different time zones, these facilities were provided round the clock. These facilities were extended by the court from time to time. But the outcome was not as spectacular as expected. It was discovered that the foreign properties were encumbered with debt from various banks and financial institutions across the world. The actual realization of money was very slow. In one case, in the state of Indiana in the US, Rs 81 crore was realized through the receiver of a local court. The matter involved sale consideration of an aircraft belonging to a subsidiary company of the group.

Sale of Indian Properties

The Indian properties had their own set of issues. Valuations given to the court in many cases had been based on the presumption of commercial use. But in Versova, Mumbai, for example, the property was in a 'no development zone' on account of it being coastal land. While Sahara valued this property at Rs 19,000 crore, it was discovered that in a consent decree in January 2012, the market value of the land paid was merely Rs 118 crores. In Vasai, Mumbai, different pieces of land were under different land-use classification. But the highest rate had been taken for the entire plot. There was the added problem that some of the title documents were not original. In Aamby Valley, which was valued by the group at approximately Rs 10,000 crore, some pieces of land had been purchased through powers of attorney, some of which were not genuine. There were litigations pending in different courts, and valuation had been done on the basis of integrated township projects. Land use remained an issue. In a Kanpur property, the land had already been sold to another person by the seller from whom Sahara had purchased it. In Anantpur, the seller had only 25 per cent share in the land sold to Sahara, but he had disposed it off as though he was a 100-per-cent-owner of the land. Sixty-three properties of Sahara City Homes were attached by the income tax authorities towards tax dues. Of these, forty-three were title deeds that had been given to SEBI. All these complications resulted in a lower realization of money. The conditions for interim bail could not be fulfilled. Subsequently, SEBI filed a petition for appointing a receiver with respect to all the assets, movable and immovable, irrespective of whether these were situated in India or outside India.

The Sahara companies informed the court that they had supplied a second list of properties worth more than Rs 20,000 crore. But it was clarified by SEBI that the first list contained the Vasai and Versova properties, and there were defects in the title and valuation of these properties, so there was no second list as such. On the request of Sahara for interim bail to be granted to Roy Sahara and others, in March 2016, the Supreme Court permitted SEBI to devise its own mechanism to dispose of the properties whose title deeds had been submitted by Sahara. The only requirement was that no property could be sold at a price less than 90 per cent of the circle rate.

As of 31 January 2018, the total money realized or received by SEBI was less than Rs 15,000 crore.[1] Sahara had been directed to deposit a principal amount of nearly Rs 25,000 crore to SEBI. This works out to be about 60 per cent of the principal amount due, without taking into account the interest liability of Sahara.

As far as the refund to investors was concerned, against a claim of more than three crore investors, the total number of applications received was 11,891, amounting to a total claim of Rs 59,55,18,203. Taking into account the cases that were disputed or not in consonance with the direction of the Supreme Court, SEBI could refund only 8551 bondholders—the principal amount of Rs 31,11,23,500 and an interest of Rs 23,50,80,385. The total amount came to Rs 54,62,03,885 or less than 3 per cent of the total amount raised by Sahara.

Parole

In May 2016, following the death of his mother, Roy was released on parole along with Roy Choudhary. Later, Dubey was also released. As of 2019, they continue to be on parole. There has been no significant increase either in the amount realized from the sale of Sahara's assets or the number of applications for refund received by SEBI. In the meanwhile, another development has taken place. Another group entity, Sahara India Commercial Corporation Ltd (SICCL), was found to have made an offer of OFCDs between 1998 and 2009 and raised an amount of more than Rs 14,000 crore from approximately two crore investors. In an order passed by SEBI in October 2018, SICCL and its directors have been asked to refund the amount, along with interest at the rate of 15 per cent. Other directions similar to the one passed in 2011, such as being debarred from dealing in the market or being associated with a listed company, have also been issued.

The fact that about 60 per cent of the principal amount has been realized or received is because of the steadfastness of the Supreme Court. Several steps were taken by the group to contest the matter in various legal forums. But the Supreme Court took several extraordinary measures, such as prohibiting all other courts and tribunals from dealing with this matter, appointing a retired Supreme Court judge to monitor the progress made by SEBI, and asking that the money be deposited with the regulator. A number of hearings took place in the Supreme Court and valuable time was spent on this matter. The biggest and the most expensive legal minds in the country appeared for Sahara at various stages. The matter attracted substantial media attention, and political leaders across parties took a keen interest in the matter. SEBI was represented by Arvind Datar.

During the meetings of the parliamentary standing committee on finance, and even outside them, questions were raised as if one business group had been targeted in a singular manner in trying to amend the SEBI Act. Attempts were made in a variety of ways, including threats of raising privilege motions in the Parliament and intimidating SEBI officials. However, it goes to the credit of successive finance ministers—Mukherjee, Chidambaram and Jaitley—that they stood their ground and didn't interfere in the matter. The ministers and the officials of the ministry of finance also deserve credit for upholding the rule of law and the morale of SEBI officials.

The fact remains that in spite of all this effort, only approximately 60 per cent of the principal amount could be realized. The actual investors who claimed refunds were in thousands instead of crores. It is one of the most important mysteries in the modern finance of the country. The Supreme Court repeatedly rejected the stand of the group that it had refunded more than two crore investors in cash and well before the Supreme Court order of 31 August 2012. The Supreme Court didn't find any merit in the claim that this payment was made in cash by divestment by another group company. If this was the outcome in the matter so seriously dealt within the Supreme Court, it is not difficult to imagine what would happen in other cases. In case of MPS Greenery Developers Ltd, SEBI had similarly witnessed media advertisements condemning it, but the ferocity of tone in the media outburst of Sahara against a legally constituted independent regulator was unprecedented. SEBI was asked to participate in a live TV debate and called a 'sarkari gunda' and aspersions were cast on its intentions.

As far as the realization of money is concerned, the percentage of realization in other cases like SRIL, Rose Valley Group, PACL and others have been very, very low, even where courts have appointed retired judges to monitor sale of assets and refund to investors.

The Lesson

The real lesson here is for regulatory agencies to remain alert right from the beginning and to take decisive preventive action. Restitution of money to investors and containing the damage later become more difficult. Multiple cases have taken more than ten to twenty years in various courts, and poor people have suffered. A multipronged approach consisting of the following may be a solution going forward:

i. Removing inter-regulatory gaps and bringing direct accountability are most critical. Based on the experience of Sahara, SRIL, PACL and many other cases, the 2014 amendment in the SEBI Act prescribed that all fund-collection schemes exceeding Rs 100 crore or more will be deemed to be a CIS and come within the jurisdiction of SEBI. This is a very welcome step.

ii. Enactment of state laws to protect the interests of the depositors has been a very successful move. It takes quite some time for an unauthorized scheme to reach the level of Rs 100 crore. Prompt and effective action under the state laws passed by almost all the state governments have proven to be very effective. States such as Maharashtra, Jharkhand and Bihar have done very good work in this matter.

iii. Regulatory coordination at the state level is absolutely essential. This helps exchange of information across regulators and governments at the operational levels well in time. The RBI has offices in all the states. SEBI has set up offices in almost all states. Arrangements made by the RBI for a state-level coordination committee (SLCC) under the chief secretary of the state have helped control these activities. But these steps are still at a nascent stage.

iv. Investors' awareness and financial literacy are the primary needs. SEBI took the initiative by having training programmes in smaller towns, and in its state-level offices. Awareness was created through audiovisual programmes. But much still needs to be done. The RBI, SEBI and MCA have their own funds for investor awareness and education. A coordinated plan involving all the agencies will help.

The recent law (2019) passed by the Parliament, which curbs unauthorized deposit-taking and provides effective measures to control such unauthorized collection, is a step in the right direction.

Instances of unauthorized deposit-collection have been recorded across the world at different points of time. In India, the practice was at its peak in the 1990s and again between 2009 and 2013. Hopefully, the measures taken by the government, the Parliament and the regulators will help avoid a repeat of such activities. But the fact remains that neither in the Sahara case nor in any other case has all the money been recovered. The Sahara case is still pending in the Supreme Court as of 2019.

PART V

Some Parting Thoughts

19

Relationship between the Government and Regulators

A public debate about the relationship between the government and regulators often ends up demonizing the government. The general belief is that the government interferes in the affairs of the regulators and compromises their independence. Having worked for a considerable period of time on both sides of the aisle, I would like to bring in my perspective on the subject.

It is the government that is responsible to the Parliament. Regulators cannot participate in its debates, except when summoned as witnesses by committees of the Parliament. The actions (or inactions) of the regulators have to be defended by the government in the Parliament. Even if attempts are made by the government to dissociate itself from these, the Parliament and the people of the country do not accept this argument at its face value. When the Harshad Mehta scam took place, the government could not pass the buck and get away by saying that the supervision of the government-bond market had been entirely in the hands of the RBI and it was not to blame. In the Ketan Parekh scam, the government could not convince the Parliament that as the securities markets are regulated by SEBI, their responsibility is very limited. As we have discussed in Chapter 2 of this book, even in the case of UTI, where the government was not a shareholder, it had no nominee of its own on the board and the UTI management had otherwise kept the government in the dark, the government could not escape its accountability.

Any responsive government receives hundreds of petitions and suggestions from the public. Most of them require consultations with the regulator. When there is a crisis or the financial stability is at stake, the government and the regulators have to mutually reinforce each other. Such situations arise in every part of the world. The global financial crisis and its huge impact may be assigned to some extent on the lack of timely and sufficient regulatory oversight, but the cleaning-up would not have taken place without the two sides working together and implementing some unprecedented measures. Similarly, political developments often overtake the normal agenda of a regulator. The Bank of England had no role in the country coming to a decision on Brexit, but it has a very significant role in dealing with the economic and monetary implications of the decision.

During the consultation process for changing the Takeover Code in 2010-11 or while designing the new SECC Regulations during 2014-15, the government, fellow regulators, trade bodies, experts and academics had a lot to suggest. Their concerns had to be taken on board and addressed. During the drafting of REITs and InvITs Regulations, important inputs from the government had to be accommodated. Often different arms of the government, such as tax authorities and the policymaking ministries, have their different perspectives, but evaluating these inputs can enrich the decision-making process. I have seen it on multiple occasions that the government is willing to be convinced and change its stand if sufficient grounds are brought to the table. There are examples to the contrary as well. I wanted to change the mutual funds regulations so that no institution could have above 10 per cent share in more than one mutual fund, but government officials were worried that this might have an immediate impact on the ownership of UTI. The worry was that SBI, PNB, BoB and LIC would be forced to sell their shares and perhaps incur a loss. They wanted a year's time to handle it smoothly. I accepted their argument and deferred the proposal. Subsequently, after a year, this proposal was rightly carried out by the SEBI board and the necessary changes were made. It is, however, disappointing that until the time of writing this, the government has not been able to ensure these four institutions sell down their shares or exit from UTI. They continue to be in violation of SEBI's regulations.

Lines of Communication

A robust line of communication between the government and the regulators is a healthy way to understand the points of view of each side, resolve differences and avoid controversies. A structured mechanism for engagement between the government and the regulators has been recommended by parliamentary committees. The Financial Stability and Development Council is one such mechanism. It needs to meet more regularly and be made more effective. I also used to have regular interactions with the secretaries in the ministries and other senior officers. In addition, one-on-one interactions between the regulatory heads, the finance minister and the prime minister once in a while are a very effective way to ensure coordination and mutual understanding. I learnt this during my days in the finance ministry. Successive governors of the RBI and chairmen of SEBI followed this time-honoured practice. Many niggling issues since a long time used to get sorted out in minutes. During my time in SEBI, I saw frequent changes in the office of the finance minister. Pranab Mukherjee was replaced by P. Chidambaram when the former became the president of India. For a brief period, when Pranab Mukherjee had resigned at the time and filed his nomination, Manmohan Singh held the additional charge of finance minister for a couple of months. After the 2014 elections, Arun Jaitley came in. All of them showed appreciation for SEBI's work and offered support from the government. Finance ministers used to visit RBI and SEBI offices once in a while. We used to make presentation on developments in the market and challenges faced by SEBI. There used to be detailed discussions in which the ministers actively participated.

I also had the occasion of having regular meetings with the two prime ministers. Manmohan Singh was proud of the fact that he had piloted the SEBI bill in the parliament. He readily agreed to our request to be the chief guest in the function to celebrate twenty-five years of SEBI. He always had some sound advice on how to balance the multiple roles of SEBI and what the main focus areas for the government are at any given time. I used to meet PM Modi once in two–three months. Whenever I met him, he always came across as being very inquisitive. His priority was to make market supervision strict. Nobody should be allowed to get away after committing irregularities; deterrent action should be taken against the perpetrators. The biggest strength was his firm belief that no person, big or small, should be spared. He was also a very keen listener to international economic and financial developments and used to ask several questions to clarify his doubts. It was heartening that he used to devote substantial amount of time during these meetings and remained fully focused on the topic. He also used to bounce off inputs received by him or ideas present in his mind and encouraged frank professional views. Many sensitive issues got resolved in these meetings.

Independence

Modern regulators are creatures of the Parliament. In the complex world of finance innovation, expertise and knowledge are required in a regulator. It also has to exhibit objectivity and reflect no bias. Regulators have to function within clearly stated policy frameworks to convey the stability and predictability of regulations to the market. Frequent reversal in regulatory approach can do more harm to the country. Independence is also required, because in many service areas government entities and the private sector compete with each other. Regulators have to take owner-neutral decisions. In corporate governance, even today there are different rules for government companies with regard to minimum public shareholding, board constitution or the appointment process of boards. Most of these can be easily done away with, but this is not taking place. These cases affect the credibility of the regulator and naturally affect their independence in the eyes of analysts, market participants (domestic or foreign), and commentators.

Another situation, which I have discussed earlier in the book, is when the mechanism of inter-regulatory coordination fails and the government is forced to intervene. This is what happened in the SEBI–IRDAI dispute regarding which agency should regulate ULIPs. Government had to bring in an ordinance to clarify the position. Evidently, such episodes harm the case for regulatory independence.

The Role of Investigative Agencies

An organization like SEBI falls within the vigilance jurisdiction of government agencies. Often complaints are received from different quarters. It stands to reason that all these complaints against officials are appropriately examined and seen through to a logical end. Some of these cases are straightforward and easy to verify, but difficulties arise when the complaints are with regard to the quasi-judicial orders passed by SEBI. Any frustrated person can complain that the quantum of punishment awarded was too low or too high or there was a deliberate delay in passing the order, thereby benefiting the offender. Quasi-judicial orders of SEBI can be appealed before SAT, which is authorized to pass its order on the process followed, the quantum of punishment and also whether there was a delay on the part of the SEBI officials. There are multiple examples of SAT expressing its views on these aspects while passing orders during appeals. Anybody dissatisfied with the order passed by SAT can go to the Supreme Court.

In spite of such well-defined checks and balances regarding the quasi-judicial orders, it is not uncommon for people to make allegations against SEBI officials before vigilance agencies. Our legal system had anticipated such situations. The Judges (Protection) Act, 1985, defines a judge to include a person empowered by the law to give a definitive judgment in legal proceedings. An officer of SEBI passing a quasi-judicial order has protection under this law. Section 23 of the SEBI Act provides further protection to its officers for actions taken in good faith. Even the then attorney general in 2015, opined that the protection under the Judges (Protection) Act extends to the officers of SEBI in discharging their quasi-judicial orders.

In spite of this, SEBI officials continued to face investigations asking them for appearance. Even searches were conducted in their houses. In one case, while hearing an appeal, SAT issued unfavourable directions against a whole-time member for delay in passing an order. Later on, these directions were withdrawn by SAT. However, based on this information published in newspapers, vigilance authorities initiated a proceeding on why this delay had taken place. This overreach has been an important area affecting the efficiency as well as the independence of the regulator. It firstly encourages a tendency to play cautious and not take any proactive steps, lest any motive is imputed. The other result could be to take the most drastic step, right from the beginning, whenever any information or complaint is received. In fact, several members of Parliament suggested to me that SEBI should pass an interim order restricting all activities of deposit-taking companies the moment a complaint is received. Often, it is difficult for people to appreciate that in quasi-judicial proceedings, there has to be strong material on record to justify interim orders of prohibition. Besides, SEBI officials have always got to keep in mind that the orders can be challenged in higher forums where their orders can be examined from a variety of angles of propriety.

Financial Independence

Financial independence is the basic requirement for the functioning of an independent regulator. A regulator should have its own source of income and the flexibility to utilize it without looking up to the government for funds. The RBI has its own sources of income and distributes dividend to government every year. The SEBI Act provides for the regulator to be able to levy fees and charges, and create its own fund. SEBI board is required to prepare its annual budget, where it can revise the rates of fees upwards and downwards based on its estimate of money required for its activities during the year. The board also has representation from the government. Besides, SEBI's accounts are audited by the CAG. There have been some recent developments to take away this freedom and ask SEBI to park its income in the Consolidated Fund of India or in the Public Account, and to seek prior approval of government before incurring any capital expenditure. Such efforts are not conducive in creating a strong and independent regulatory environment. All other regulators must have their own sources of income and not survive on the receipt of grants from the government.

Internal Independence

Independence of the regulator should not be defined only with regard to independence from the government and its officials. It is also to be seen in the context of independence from any outside influences, including those from market participants and business corporations. There has been worry about market capture of regulators in other parts of the world. The senior leadership and the board of regulators have to remain extra-cautious on this account. At the same time, remaining insulated from the market is not the solution.

Another dimension of independence is internal independence. Although, the law permits this, the quasi-judicial function of SEBI needs to be separated from executive supervision. When the SEBI Act was passed in 1992, there may have been some justification for this arrangement because of lack of capacity and trained manpower. But now this needs to be revisited. In other countries, such a separation does exit. The possibilities of an adjudicating officer getting transferred to an executive or policy role in the future does affect his judgement while adjudicating matters. It may be recalled that with the 2014 amendment of the SEBI Act, orders passed by an adjudication officer can be appealed before SEBI in certain cases. As such, maintaining institutional consistency in identical or similar matters is now possible through a quasi-judicial process. A separate cadre of officers performing quasi-judicial functions needs to be developed. This also applies to whole-time members passing quasi-judicial orders. There should be whole-time members earmarked for this work, while other members can perform executive and policy functions.

Multiplicity of Regulators

Since liberalization, twenty regulators covering the financial, economic and infrastructure sectors have been set up in the country. These vary from SEBI to Telecom Regulatory Authority of India (TRAI), to Coastal Aquaculture Authority (CAA) to IBBI. While there is a need for institutions that are experts in their respective areas, such a diverse arrangement creates difficulty for monitoring and coordination.

In the FSDC committee and High Level Coordination Committee on Financial Markets (HLCCFM) that I have been observing for two decades, there used to be four to five participants in the beginning. Now, there are more than fifteen participants. The meetings have become mere formalities. Between the RBI and SEBI, we had developed our own informal arrangements which worked very well. When Raghuram Rajan became the governor of RBI, we developed a system of visiting each other and having meetings every six to eight weeks. We used to have agendas set in advance. Most of the outstanding issues could be resolved in this manner. Several developments in the bond market, FPIs, currency derivatives, risk management in clearing corporations or development of new derivative products took place as a result of these meetings. The practice continued when Urjit Patel became the governor.

Consultation

One point of friction that often arises is the belief of the government that regulators are not responsive, the representation made has been cast aside, or the public has not been given the opportunity to be heard. Naturally, such an individual or organization would then approach the government. It has been my experience that if the regulator is transparent and has a mechanism to interact with the industry as well as the people having grievances, such a situation can be avoided. I have seen that often impressions about the regulator being insular or unresponsive are wrongly created. SEBI has a long tradition of having advisory committees on areas such as mutual funds, primary markets, etc. My approach was that at the beginning of the meetings I would meet the chairman and members, express SEBI's concerns and leave them for deliberations. I refrained from participating in the meetings of these advisory committees. That ensured that discussions were free and frank. SEBI's officials were often challenged in these meetings. Different points of views were brought in. It is through this mechanism that the mutual funds advisory committee under Janki Ballabh or primary market advisory committee under T.V. Mohandas Pai could help SEBI bring about reforms in these areas.

SEBI also started the practice of meeting different professional groups such as lawyers, merchant bankers, brokers or credit-rating agencies once in six months, or even more frequently, if needed. SEBI used to furnish action-taken reports, ATRs on the discussions in previous meetings. The professional groups were surprised at such openness from SEBI. These interactions have helped SEBI bring in timely reforms and avoid costly mistakes.

Reforms in the Government

There is also the issue of the lack of expert knowledge in the government. During Chidambaram's time as finance minister, we had started a system of an informal advisory group for the finance minister. It consisted of five–six other experts from different segments of the market. The meeting used to take place at frequent intervals without the presence of the regulator in the meeting. This led to frank and fearless inputs and a much better understanding of the market, its issues and international developments. This helped in the ministry's future discussions with SEBI.

The appointment and removal of senior-level functionaries in regulatory bodies would also benefit from transparency. Often the law is silent, the rules are vague and the process is rushed. This raises questions about the independence of the regulator and future objectivity in its decisions. The powers of removal have been provided to the government under various laws. The government is also empowered to issue directions to regulators. Governments have to be given credit for showing restraint in exercising these powers, but some recent developments have raised concerns about the direction in which we are moving.

Accountability

Independence and accountability go hand in hand. In SEBI we engaged on our own a reputed agency to study and provide an assessment of SEBI's regulatory impact. Teams were formed to make improvements in the identified areas. International organizations also carry out an assessment programme. The IMF–World Bank Financial Sector Assessment Program (FSAP) conducts its assessment at periodic intervals. It is a matter of great satisfaction for SEBI that in the FSAP report of 2017, they have commended SEBI for the reform measures taken by it.

All regulatory bodies have a board. It is important that heads of these bodies should practise transparency and show respect to the views of the board members, some of whom are part-time members. I had proposed to the SEBI board that at least once in a year there should be a meeting of part-time and ex-officio members of the SEBI board who could call any official and discuss any issue where no whole-time member or chairman should be present. The Financial Sector Legislative Reforms Commission (FSLRC) headed by Justice B.N. Srikrishna had gone in-depth into this issue. Today, there is no satisfactory arrangement for a performance appraisal of a regulator like SEBI. The media does it. The government does it through the presence of their representatives in the SEBI board or while answering questions in the Parliament. Regulations formulated by SEBI are required to be placed before the Parliament at the earliest. The Parliament has the right to reject or modify, but the same never happens. Hardly any subordinate legislation gets modified or rejected. The Parliamentary committee on subordinate legislation has a huge task of reviewing not only the regulation framed by the multiple regulators but also the rules framed by the various ministries under different laws. In order to help them perform this task on a structured and continuous basis, substantial capacity has to be created in this committee and in other committees of Parliament. Parliamentary supervision over the regulators is a superior option to ensure accountability. The standing committees of Parliament for different ministries may have to take up this responsibility in a regular and structured way.

Acknowledgements

The idea of this book germinated in the minds of my colleagues in SEBI, then working closely with me. Friends in the media also encouraged me. The idea continued to grow in my mind, but I wanted a reasonable time to elapse after my leaving SEBI and a certain detachment to develop before taking up this exercise. When I started writing, Ajay Tyagi—my successor as chairman, SEBI—was kind enough to provide all relevant support. I owe him, Ananta Barua, Muralidhar Rao, Amarjeet Singh, Sharat Malik, Barnali Mukherjee, Prabhas Rath, Anubhav Roy and many other SEBI officials for assisting me with facts and perspective, and readily clarifying doubts.

Amongst those who had worked with me in SEBI, but are no longer associated with it, Rajiv Agarwal, Prashant Saran, S. Raman, J. Ranganayakulu and Gyan Bhushan have been very supportive. Friends in the ministry of finance, with whom I had interacted during my association before and after coming to SEBI, were also very encouraging. A sincere thanks to all of them.

I am thankful to the entire Penguin Random House team for remaining patient with me and guiding me continuously. My special thanks to Lohit Jagwani, Roshini Dadlani, Milee Ashwarya, Manasvi Madan, Sanjeeta and Joseph Antony for their tireless efforts and advice.

My family members have not only been supportive but also been regularly challenging me as the writing progressed. Upasana, my daughter-in-law, came up with the title of the book and also helped in the ideation on the design of the book cover. My wife, Shabnam, and my sons, Utkarsh and Suharsh—and his wife, Mrinalini—remained a great source of strength throughout the writing of the book. Without their encouragement, this book would not have been possible.

Notes

Chapter 2: Handling the UTI Crisis

1. 'JPC Report on Stock Market Scam and Matters Relating Thereto, 13th Lok Sabha, Vol-1', presented to Rajya Sabha on 2002, Lok Sabha Secretariat, New Delhi, p. 356, para 15.9.
2. Ibid., p. 373, para 17.3 (V).
3. Ibid., p. 366, para 16.57 (IV).
4. Ibid., p. 348, para 16.16.

Chapter 3: Ministry of Finance (Capital Markets Division)

1. 'Anand Rathi vs Securities and Exchange Board of . . . on 28 February, 2002', Sl no. 7, Indian Kanoon, https://bit.ly/2rfAiyO
2. 'National Pension System', Wikipedia, https://bit.ly/35mpLRc. Last accessed on 22 November 2019.
3. G.N. Bajpai, *A Game Changer's Memoir* (New Delhi: Random House India, 2018), p. 107.
4. Ibid.

Chapter 5: The Regulatory Architecture

1. Writ Petition (Civil) No. 374 of 2012, Supreme Court Judgment (Judge: Justice Surinder Singh Nijjar), *Arun Kumar Agrawal vs Union of India & Ors*, p. 84.

Chapter 6: Mutual Funds

1. 'Research and Information', Association of Mutual Funds in India website, https://bit.ly/2rcPrRi

Chapter 7: The Corporate Bond Market

1. Information sourced from SEBI.

Chapter 14: Corporate Governance

1. Aarti Kumari, Harpreet Singh and Manish Bansal, 'Corporate Governance in Indian Context', *International Journal of 360 Management Review*, vol. 6, no. 2, October 2018, p. 214, para 2, https://bit.ly/35v8QMx

Chapter 15: Collecting Deposits from the Public

1. '21st Report of the Standing Committee on Finance (2015-16)', Lok Sabha Secretariat, New Delhi, p. 24, para 30).

Chapter 16: Some Big Fish

1. In 2003. SEBI Order under Section 11B, 3B, 2011.
2. 'Protection of Interests of Depositors (in Financial Establishments) Act, 2018', India Code, https://bit.ly/2D4WpL1

Chapter 17: Deemed Public Issue—Sahara

1. Sandeep Bamzai, 'Sahara supremo Subrata Roy's firms barred from raising funds', *India Today*, 30 December 1999, https://bit.ly/339lOxF
2. Tamal Bandyopadhyay, *Sahara – The Untold Story* (Mumbai: Jaico Publishing House, 2014), p. 12.
3. Sachin P. Mampatta, 'Let's fight it out on TV, Sahara challenges Sebi', *Business Standard*, 17 March 2013.
4. Times News Network, 'Subrata Roy compares Sebi with "sarkari gunda"', *The Times of India*, 30 November 2013, https://bit.ly/35qU49r

Chapter 18: The Tightening Noose

1. Information sourced from SEBI.